THE PICTURE OF ADDICTION

THE PICTURE OF ADDICTION

It Can Happen to Anyone

MARGARET J. LOEWEN, MD

Foreword by Gail Janzen Newel, MD

RESOURCE *Publications* · Eugene, Oregon

THE PICTURE OF ADDICTION
It Can Happen to Anyone

Resource Publications
An Imprint of Wipf and Stock Publishers
199 W. 8th Ave., Suite 3
Eugene, OR 97401
www.wipfandstock.com

PAPERBACK ISBN: 979-8-3852-1735-9
HARDCOVER ISBN: 979-8-3852-1736-6
EBOOK ISBN: 979-8-3852-1737-3

VERSION NUMBER 07/29/24

Received permission from Gail Janzen Newel, MD, MPH, FACOG, to publish the artwork by Nyeland Janzen Newel
Received permission to reprint "Child Diving" from Jean Janzen
Reprinted by permission of Taylor & Francis Ltd., "The Clinical Opiate Withdrawal Scale"
Received permission from CA Bridge to use "Emergency Department Buprenorphine (Bup) Quick Start"

This is a self-portrait by Nyeland Janzen Newel whose goal in life was to make the world a kinder and more beautiful place. He lived from 1978–2016, and we miss him.

CONTENTS

FOREWORD: REMEMBERING NYELAND

His younger brother found him, unresponsive, sitting slumped over on the floor of his bedroom in our home. He called 9-1-1, attempted CPR, opened the door for the paramedics a few minutes later. Our family home by the beach, a retreat for us after long days of work, was suddenly transformed into seeming chaos. The paramedic team rushed in, took over CPR, and gave the first dose of naloxone. IV lines were placed, an endotracheal tube, more naloxone, epinephrine.

Our younger son, having handed over his CPR efforts, texted us: "Nyeland overdosed. The paramedics are here."

I froze, shocked and helpless. I was three hours from home, preparing to give the keynote address at a conference the following morning. My wife, who worked nearby, rushed home from her medical office to find our normally quiet street lit up with the flashing lights of a fire truck, Sheriff's car and ambulance. She ran in and took in the scene, a parent's worst nightmare. She was still in her scrubs, her hospital badge still in place: Kelli Beingesser, MD, Obstetrics and Gynecology. One of the paramedics looked up at her in recognition and said, "Hi Dr. B, so sorry this is happening," before turning back to Nyeland. After five doses of naloxone and multiple rounds of advanced cardiopulmonary resuscitation, a heartbeat. A glimmer of hope. The paramedic team loaded him into the ambulance and raced to the nearest emergency department. Despite best efforts, my first-born son, Nyeland, was declared dead shortly after arrival, another opioid overdose in a hospital growing accustomed to such tragedies.

This is why Dr. Margaret Loewen's book is so important—addiction and its impacts can happen to anyone, including healthcare professionals and their families. Here she tells the story of her own education in addiction, both personal and professional, then offers practical guidance as well as hope. It is a call to action at a time when we are losing far too many precious and valuable lives, lives with the potential to thrive for decades longer, to contribute productively, to participate fully in our communities.

Margaret and I have both experienced the trauma of addiction, in our work and in our homes. We have shared similar walks of life from the time we became friends in childhood and as we each decided to pursue medicine as a career. Soon after Nyeland's death, Margaret approached me with the idea of writing a book together about our shared experiences. I was enthusiastic. Each of us had our own areas of professional expertise in the field of addiction: Margaret's in direct care in emergency settings, mine in population-level public health. But when I sat down to write, my grief was too raw, the wound too fresh. I am grateful that Margaret persisted, and that this book is finally coming to fruition. None too soon, as opioid overdose deaths have just surpassed COVID deaths as the deadliest event in US history, deadlier than the HIV epidemic, the Civil War and the 1918 flu epidemic.

Nyeland Janzen Newel died on September 29, 2016, just a few days after his 38th birthday. We had celebrated his birthday together as a family the week before, on Maui, where Kelli and I were attending a medical conference. Our two sons, Nyeland and his younger brother Conlin, had joined us there, snorkeling, swimming, reconnecting with each other after time apart. Conlin had just graduated from college as a business major and was back home with us while he worked to get his own business going.

Nyeland, a dentist, had taken a week off from his work with our local non-profit dental clinic, Dientes. He loved his work there, serving our community's most vulnerable – those experiencing homelessness, undocumented workers, uninsured families. The kids were his favorite, and he had a special way of making them laugh with silly faces and jokes. He made custom stickers to share with his patients and staff. His Spanish was excellent, and he enjoyed using it on the job. His colleagues and support staff loved him. But underneath his seeming happiness and success, he was struggling.

Nyeland had moved back home to live with us a few months before his death. He had been lonely after his divorce, working for a corporate dental chain several states away from his family and support network. We were thrilled to have him close to us. Our home was on the beautiful California coast and had plenty of room for both of our adult sons and the two of us. Along with our two dogs and a cat, we were a happy household, cooking and eating dinners together, taking walks on the beach, enjoying weekends and evenings in each other's company. Nyeland had been in recovery from drugs and alcohol for many years, and, as is common, had had relapses along the way. We knew enough about addiction to know that he was at risk for using again, particularly opioids, and we watched for the signs. Nyeland professed sobriety to us. He was meditating, reading NA and AA materials, journaling, and seeming to walk the walk. Kelli was also in recovery, from alcohol, and the two of them went to AA meetings together on a regular basis. As physicians, we had both had professional training in addition to our personal experiences with alcoholism and addiction. In a two-physician household, how could this happen? If it could happen to us, it can happen to anyone.

My own understanding of addiction has come through painful, personal experience. Alcoholism, addiction and the other diseases of despair have been only superficially taught in traditional healthcare curricula, despite their enormous impact on the health and wellbeing of our nation. The stigma associated with these diseases has kept them under wraps, even as we struggle with their consequences in our daily lives. I was fortunate to have a better than average medical school education in the field of addiction, but it was not until I personally experienced its effects that I began to grasp the enormity of its impact. My career transition from clinical medicine to public health drove the message home: I was not the only parent to have lost a child to this terrible disease, I was not the only doctor to have experienced the personal tragedy of addiction, and we were not the only family wounded by its impacts. This was, and continues to be, an epidemic. As a Health Officer during the COVID pandemic, I watched the opioid deaths in my own community spike as the COVID death numbers ticked upward. In neighboring San Francisco, there were times in the pandemic that the opioid overdose deaths exceeded the COVID deaths.

Opioid overdose death rates throughout our nation continue to climb, year after year, resulting in more years of lost life than from any other cause of death. This is a tragedy impacting our children, our families and our communities. We must take action. How do we tackle the problem of addiction? There is no easy answer. It will require collaboration across many sectors, including healthcare, behavioral health, law enforcement, criminal justice, social services and legislators. Our schools, workplaces, houses of worship and community groups must be involved. We must utilize primary and secondary prevention approaches as well as treatment. It will take time and persistence. This book offers a place to start in the healthcare setting, including step-by-step programmatic approaches and references for further information and assistance. For that I am grateful for Margaret's willingness to push through her own pain to tell her family's story and to bring this book to print. I hope you find it useful as you join the effort to save lives and relieve the suffering of those impacted by addiction.

Gail Janzen Newel, MD, MPH, FACOG
Obstetrician-Gynecologist
Public Health Officer
Nyeland's mother

ACKNOWLEDGMENTS

THE AUTHOR WISHES TO thank many who encouraged, taught and shared their knowledge as this writing project developed over a period of many years. Early on, Mary Sanichas helped bolster my courage to persist, then came to my rescue with her talent, skill, and effort in creating the images associated with Appendix 3. My cousin Faith Eidse shared with me her knowledge and experience as an author. She was willing to become my writing coach as this manuscript began to take shape in preparation for publication.

Our family thanks the family of Jodi Rae Maestas for allowing us to tell the story of her beautiful life and tragic death. My son Bez and I hope that in the writing of this book we can reduce further unnecessary loss of life due to stigma and resistance to treat the disease of opioid use disorder.

The experiences of the family of Nyeland Janzen Newel parallel that of the Maestas family, having also lost a loved one to this brutal disease at almost the same time. The contribution of Dr. Gail Janzen Newel, mother of Nyeland, by providing resources that are shared in this book in addition to her family's story, helps the reader better understand this disease. "Remembering Nyeland," demonstrates how widespread is the grief and loss as a result of the opioid epidemic. Jean Janzen, grandmother of Nyeland, has been a special person in my life since I was 17 years old. She became a renowned poet when she pursued higher education after raising her four children and while supporting her wonderful pediatrician husband, Dr. Louis Janzen. Her poem, "Child Diving," was written for her grandson Nyeland. When I lived with the family of Louis and Jean Janzen during my senior year of high school, their peaceful and creative home helped me imagine greater possibilities for my life than what I had known and I thank them.

Finally, I want to express my gratitude for the kind and gentle person who was my husband. Bob Yoder was my sweet, calming influence who kept me going forward in spite of the many difficulties that our family faced over the years that we were married. He had many talents that he was willing to share with anyone who was willing to learn. He died before this book was published but his spirit lives in the words on these pages. All the meals he cooked for me, all the sporting events and old movies we watched together, all the love he gave me, our sons, our daughter-in-law and our three granddaughters will never be forgotten.

ABBREVIATIONS AND DEFINITIONS

ALTO | alternatives to opioids

APP | advanced practice provider who can be a nurse practitioner or physician assistant with extra training to provide direct care for patients

BID | two times daily

BUP | buprenorphine

CO | carbon monoxide

CO_2 | carbon dioxide

EMTALA | Emergency Medical Treatment and Labor Act requiring medical screening and stabilizing treatment of all patients who come to the ER regardless of ability to pay

ER or ED | emergency department

HIPPA | Health Insurance Portability and Accountability Act of 1996, a federal law designed to protect sensitive patient health information from being disclosed without the patient's consent or knowledge

Induction | the starting of buprenorphine in medication assisted treatment of OUD

JAMA | The Journal of the American Medical Association

IV | intravenous

kg | kilogram, equals one thousand grams which is 2.2 pounds

MAT | medication assisted treatment

meth | methamphetamine

mcg	microgram, equals one millionth of a gram
mg	milligram, equals one thousandth of a gram
NEJM	The New England Journal of Medicine
opiate	Natural derivative from the opium poppy plant
opioid	Refers to drugs that are natural and semi-synthetic derivatives of the opium poppy as well as similar synthetic compounds that have analgesic or pain relieving properties because of their effects in the central nervous system . . . Opioids are often inappropriately referred to as narcotics, a legal term that is no longer used in medicine because it suggests that opioids relieve pain by inducing sedation; while sedation can be a side effect of opioids, it is not the mechanism that produces pain relief.[1]
OUD	opioid use disorder
PCP	primary care provider
PO	per oral—that is, medication taken by mouth
Pt	patient
Q	every
Rx	prescription
SL	sublingual
TID	three times daily
Tx	treatment
>	greater than
<	less than

---

1. Fishman, *Responsible Opioid Prescribing*, 5.

Part I

A PERSONAL STORY OF FIGHTING BACK
IN SMALL TOWN AMERICA

Chapter 1

BEFORE 2010—BLENDING CAREER AND FAMILY

I WAS PROBABLY MORE than a little nuts when I decided to head down this career path later in life than anyone I knew. Reminded by a special friend while catching up over lunch that I had been unusually old when I started medical school, I was startled by the comment but nodded at her from across the table. Munching on my cold pork and olive sandwich, I bought myself some time to think by contemplating the antique pattern on the high ceiling of the picturesque Greek restaurant. Listening to the echoing chatter of patrons with the short-order cook behind the counter, I had to admit she was right. I remembered that many years earlier she had supported her husband through his years of training to become a pediatrician. It occurred to me that Jean understood better than anyone what this decision meant in its varied complexities for me and my family.

She asked me a very simple question, "Why?"

The soft features of her face were framed by shoulder length light brown hair and her blue eyes were expressing something akin to concern, demonstrated by a slight squint as she intently watched me.

I tried but couldn't define the reasons well enough in my mind to verbalize an honest reply. At that time, it was still early in my own understanding of the new opportunities and life I would have as a medical doctor after having worked for twenty years in the professional realm of human nutrition. Emotions and conflicting motivations made it impossible for me to distill these thoughts into a coherent answer. I couldn't do any more than promise to tell her when I had it figured out.

"I will give you an update someday when I can answer this question," I said lamely. She appeared to be disappointed with my inability to articulate my reasoning but offered me her support as she always did. Her unconditional love was a constant.

Years later, I began to realize that one of the factors contributing to the decision that she and I had been discussing was that I had a lot to prove. I had grown up at a time when higher education for women was encouraged but a demanding career was not. Chafing against the cultural norms, I had found my way out of a restricted space.

I had pushed tradition aside already, marrying a man who held similar values as my own in many respects. But he lacked an appreciation for my closely held ideals of nonviolence which were non-negotiable. The strength of my feelings on this score were doubtless related to terrifying memories from childhood that I could never forget.

When I was ten years old, my parents, siblings and I had experienced 111 days as hostages in Stanleyville. This was the largest city in the northern part of what had been the Belgian Congo. In 1964 this newly independent country was convulsed in a civil war. An uprising occurred after the fledgling democracy suffered political interference due to an effort by their former colonial master to control its alliances, purportedly in cooperation with the CIA. The Democratic Republic of Congo's first prime minister, elected to lead this young nation, was Patrice Lumumba, a charismatic man revered by the Congolese to this day. His unexplained death during a routine flight across this mineral rich tropical country, for which all foreign governments denied responsibility, caused immense grief for this nation, justifiable anger, and a passionate distrust of the Belgians and Americans. That my father was a Canadian was fortunate. Neither American nor Belgian, he was an administrator for a Congolese university located in the center of this conflict. His job apparently conferred some protection for us during those months of occupation by the rebel soldiers who were also known as the Simbas. Our family was not harmed physically during our captivity. This was not the case for far too many Congolese, possibly as many as half a million, and hundreds of Belgians and Americans as well as expatriates of other nationalities who lost their lives during this civil war. No surprise, I detest guns and violence.

In addition to this personal history, the pacifist culture of my ancestors did not blend seamlessly with the pugilistic culture of my husband who had grown up in the mountains of Appalachia. Given our differences, perhaps the eventual demise of our marriage was predictable. However, for me, marrying Henry had been a liberating choice because this was a relationship filled with freedom that allowed me to learn and grow.

When my husband and I discovered our infertility after seven years of marriage we were thrilled beyond words to adopt a newborn baby boy. As our first baby grew into childhood, like other adoptive parents we discovered that the natural talents of this lovely child were in some ways strikingly different from our own. I always remarked to myself with amazement that even as a preschooler little Frankie would never forget a face or a name, a trait that stands out among his natural abilities to this day. This was a gift he had received from his genetic inheritance, not a result of any training he had gotten from us. Quite honestly, neither Henry nor I were talented socially.

When we were able to adopt a second time, we were absolutely in heaven. There was an eight-year age gap between our sons who both joined our family when they were newborns. They were beautiful beyond words in all the ways that children should be in the hearts and minds of their parents. For me, these precious children brought fulfillment and so much joy. In addition, Frankie was grateful to have a little brother when he finally arrived! Despite the years between them, these boys were close, they were bonded. Little Bezzy completed our family in such a perfect way.

However, within our nuclear family dark clouds were forming on the horizon. The wind was whipping up and some shrill tones were unmistakable when I listened carefully for meaning. In an effort to make things better for my family, it seemed like a change of some kind was needed. I was apparently the only one in our marital partnership perceiving the threat. Cracks in our union were beginning to appear. As a result, one fateful day I had an epiphany at work and when I returned home that evening, I proposed starting a career in medicine. I received only encouragement from Henry. He thought it was a wonderful idea and he cheered me on. This was why I started medical school at the age of forty-seven.

Unconventional life choices for a Mennonite girl might lead to countless challenges in personal relationships and I can confirm that many interesting situations did precede the events described in this book. Although I had loved the man that I married at least in part because of a different perspective that he offered me, there were dramatic differences between our two learned cultures. These differences could be accommodated before our children arrived but afterward, they simply couldn't be ignored. We worked with several family therapists, in succession. We tried very hard to be parents together with years of supreme effort given to compromise. We talked through differences in our views of what we each considered appropriate child rearing, but in the end we could not succeed. To be brief and much to my surprise since I never thought I was a quitter, our marriage had to come to an end for the physical and emotional safety of our children. I hated that this was the ultimate result of twenty-five years of living in a veritable two-culture household. I felt like a failure.

I am not going to minimize the effect of the divorce on my family in the telling of this story. It was complicated and difficult to share the truth with worried family members and friends when I left Henry with the children in tow. The problem was that I literally had to get my children out of that home environment before someone got killed. When I hear about family violence and murder-suicides I can relate to that unthinkable level of conflict within a family that often is so well concealed that even close friends and relatives are unaware. I considered leaving medical school briefly but decided that my need to focus on an intense educational program was not the source of the conflict. I kept going down this path because it would ultimately provide a level of financial security that I would not have if I left before completing the program. This seemed best for the future of my children and myself to continue pursuing the medical degree. When I was prepared for what I had to do we literally drove away one day. Sitting in the car together with my boys in the back seat, headed to my brother's house, I told the children we were leaving and not going back. They both cheered.

Our oldest son Frank was graduating from high school when we separated but our second son Bezzy continued to live with me. Although Bez and I had moved from a small northern Midwestern town to a different city during the last years of my medical education, we were fortunate to find neighbors there whose loving ways as a family made it possible for him to enjoy their love and attention while I was almost endlessly studying and working in hospitals to gain my clinical experience. With the start of my residency program, Bez and I moved again to a city not far from our town of origin, and in this neighborhood, we made new friends again who also bonded wonderfully with us. In our condo neighborhood an older woman and her adult daughter provided friendship, companionship, and eyes while others I hired to be present in our home were making sure Bez had appropriate supervision in my absence. Bezzy and these wonderful neighborhood friends worked on decorating projects and crafts that taught him much about creating beauty. In addition, he was also happy to have access to a swimming pool where he perfected his swimming skills while being watched by his nanny.

Thinking back to these years, this sweet youngster was doing well. He attended a public school in a district with a lot of resources providing him with many opportunities that enriched his life. He was especially digging learning to play the saxophone! What a gift that was for his development. He had started taking piano lessons when I was in medical school but, unfortunately, with my even more demanding schedule in residency I could not keep this up. Clearly, he had a talent for musical improvisation as well as artistry. I had chosen a safe and friendly neighborhood when we moved to this new urban environment. Aware of Bez's need for a good support system in this location where we didn't have any family or longtime friends, it was important to provide him with a great school district. That I had the means to provide this for him, I am still thankful.

He made some good friends his own age whose parents liked him and recognized his need to connect socially. One of his closest friends was a boy whose mother was an administrator for the Girl Scouts national organization and Bez was invited to be their guest when they went to the Great Wolf Lodge for a short family vacation. It was quite a gift. Bez was well liked and seemed happy generally. We had joined a local congregation, and he went through the normal religious teaching for a young person of his age.

But as with every child, there were difficulties too.

One of the hardest things during this period in his life was when his special little dog came up missing. He had an adventurous pet who could squeeze through the tiniest opening in the sliding door of our walkout basement and given the slightest opportunity the dog would take off. One weekend Bez and I were out of town visiting family and upon our return we discovered that the furry creature had escaped and had not returned. Bez was devastated. This little dog was never found, and it was a significant loss for him as well as a cause for longstanding grief. I don't know if he has completely resolved that sadness, even now. My priority of meeting ongoing medical residency requirements prevented me from taking time off to locate the lost animal.

Another situation occurred when he was about thirteen. He and a friend from our neighborhood were caught stealing something from a local store. I had gotten an urgent call at work from a supervisor at that retail establishment telling me that the store's security staff had called the police. Bez and the girl were charged with theft. I was stunned. I rushed to the store as soon as I could leave work and found that he and his friend were being held in a small dark, windowless room with cinderblock walls painted a depressing shade of blue. It was memorable to me in its ominous appearance. It was a stark room with a bare light bulb providing some dim light.

Both were sitting quietly in metal chairs lined up against one wall. Bez was not very forthcoming with information; it seemed to me that he was attempting to appear nonchalant about the whole situation which was un-derstandable since he was sitting next to his also accused friend. However, he did look pale and serious, staring off in another direction that did not connect with my eyes. He was almost wordless during the conversation we had with the police officer and the store manager. In the end, he and the girl were banned from that store forever and the juvenile authorities sentenced him to several months of weekly classes with his peers.

My gorgeous youngest child with a heart of gold who wanted nothing more than to make the people that he loved happy, was becoming increas-ingly distressed with his father's incessant raging against the world of his mother's family and friends. On Christmas Eve, Bez ran into my parents' house with tears coursing down his cheeks after being dropped off by his dad as my extended family was assembling for the annual celebration and gift exchange around the tree, beautifully decorated for this season.

I asked, after pulling Bez into a private space, "What's wrong? What has happened?"

"Dad's gonna kill Lee!" he shouted.

Eyes puffy from crying, he was frantic. His youthful lanky arms were waving at me for emphasis as he shouted, "Call the police!"

That was when it became completely clear to me that I needed to get help from the courts. Lee and I had been dating after my divorce and my ex was not accepting that our marriage was over. I didn't have money to spare on my resident's salary, but I also didn't have a choice. My lawyer filed the complaint that allowed for a hearing. The judge ruled in my favor and my ex was required to attend court-ordered parenting training and anger management classes. Meanwhile, Henry was not allowed any unsupervised visits while his behavior was being closely monitored. When he demon-strated his improvement in conversations and activities with our son, the restrictions gradually lifted and they were allowed to be together again, unsupervised.

I was a single mother, and I was doing my best for my dependent children. It was so over the top for me emotionally to be in court fighting for my son's sanity and for my family's safety during that time. Henry's threats of violence were eye-opening for me even though I was well-read. I had certainly experienced compassion for other women who had been through similar difficulties - I just never thought it would happen to me. The conflict between my family's needs and my requirements at work were almost more than I could manage. But I was not a quitter. That is what I told myself every day, in fact several times a day when it was especially rough going.

"I am not a quitter."

The drama between my ex and myself certainly contributed to some of Bez's anxiety and I blamed what seemed to be acting out behaviors on these unsettling events in our family. Eventually, the tension subsided.

Both Frankie and Bezzy had gotten to know Lee over several years and the relationship between them had grown. My boys became our boys when these two youngsters were witnesses at our wedding. I married Lee who was from a similar culture as my own. He was a friend from college days who was about done with his own career and wanted to help me with mine. He did help me and our children in very significant ways, including keeping us afloat financially during my residency and by encouraging me to keep going with my post-doctoral training. Our two children needed him, and they also grew to love him.

However, over the next few years more episodes of impulsive behavior by Bez left me puzzled. These were not outside the realm of normal development, I suppose, but still concerning to me as a mother. One day some old coins stored in my new in-laws' basement went missing. My ex contacted me and told me that Bez had brought them over to show him these treasures. I checked with my in-laws, and they confirmed what my ex suspected, that Bez had taken them without permission.

I flat out asked Bez, "Why did you take these coins?"

"Because I wanted them," he said.

His answer did not demonstrate remorse or regret, which surprised me.

Meanwhile, some of his teachers at school were letting me know that his work was not getting completed and they requested an evaluation for attention deficit hyperactivity disorder. I filled out the questionnaire that was designed for the parental input portion of the evaluation and the teachers also completed theirs. A child psychologist diagnosed ADHD and Ritalin was recommended. I agreed that it would be worth a try. At first Bez was cooperative with taking it. His focus improved, his performance and grades demonstrated better results, and he needed less help getting his homework done. It was an important step that helped him academically, but it didn't reassure me that all was well.

When I look back at the life of my youngest son in those years, I can honestly say that Bez was a very well-loved child. But the transition to the reality of divorce was tough. There was never any doubt in anyone's mind that he was bonded to me as well as any biologically born child could have been. His adoptive dad who was my ex-husband adored him as well and the fact that Bez did not share our genetics had always been a non-issue for us as parents. He was our second son. We had never introduced him as our adopted child because quite frankly to us it was irrelevant.

I had hoped to continue to work in the same community where I had been trained but it was not to be. Everyone in our family was affected by the change in my work environment that was required to continue a clinical career after residency. It was a huge decision to leave the state where I had been trained. It would mean uprooting Bez again, now halfway through high school. To minimize the changes, his dad thought it would be best if Bez would move in with him rather than move west with me and Lee. At the time of my writing this, I don't regret choosing to pursue clinical medicine, but I do regret making my youngest son's life more difficult, and I wish I could have better anticipated what was coming.

I originally went to medical school with the goal of living and practicing medicine in a small town. It hadn't occurred to me that this community might be in a different state. Certainly, moving was not difficult or new for me since I had been a missionary kid in Congo from before my earliest memory until I was 13 years old. We moved more times than I could easily count between Belgium, Congo, the Ivory Coast, Canada, and the United States. It certainly was not what I wanted for my children since I had experienced that pain of loneliness and displacement myself. I really felt like a jerk doing this to my own kid! The decision was a tug-of-war between my wish to practice clinical medicine in that rural setting and my desire to do the right thing for my youngest child.

As it turned out, when I interviewed for the job that brought us to the remote community that became our home Lee and I drove four hours in a rental car from Denver to reach this destination. It was August, the hottest month of the year. We saw a sparsely populated, nearly desert-like landscape with a lot of dusty, wind-blown sage brush. There were isolated homes inhabited by cattle-ranching families and their hardworking laborers. Occasionally, we glided past ghost towns that were boarded up, whispering of intolerable hardship, reminding me of western movie sets that I had seen in my youth when visiting in southern California. But more impressive were the endless miles of grasslands and a scrappy patchwork of hardy vegetation interrupted by colorful rocks jutting up towards the incredibly beautiful cloudless blue sky. The horizon stretched untold miles in all directions. The only trees visible were either dead or severely stressed by the constant dry winds. The trees that still sprouted green here and there owed their lives to a narrow stream of residual mountain water, a natural spring, or a longstanding irrigation canal.

The mountains that I had expected when invited to interview in Lamar receded into the distance after we left the airport. Instead of mountains, we saw wild antelope munching on sparse vegetation, dwarfed by an immense open landscape. Long-distance truckers hauled giant wind turbine blades, ranchers drove heavily built pick-up trucks and a few like us seemed to be professional travelers. Surprising to me at that time, there were few, if any, tourists.

After three hours of steady driving, I realized the area was remote enough to put a traveler at a reduced chance of survival should a motor vehicle crash occur on this stretch of the two-lane highway at these speeds. That was a sobering thought as we approached the town where we might live. My residency training at a Level 1 Trauma Center was fresh in my mind. This awareness, it might be fair to say hyperawareness, led me to calculate how long it would take a crash victim to receive stabilizing medical care should there be a serious, or worse, catastrophic injury. Per my estimation at that time, transporting a patient to an emergency department would take more than one hour in most cases.

The trimodal death distribution is a concept taken from the manual which is an industry standard for emergency physicians and trauma surgeons, titled *Advanced Trauma Life Support*. Its goals are based on the importance of optimizing the quality of medical treatment during. . . "The golden hour of care after injury. . . ." [1] Rapid transport to a specialized trauma center is associated positively with survival of a serious injury. Delay of care is deadly. The compelling results of decades of research had been stressed repeatedly during residency and there was a warning bell ringing

1. Rotondo, *Advanced Trauma Life Support*, xxv.

in my head that I could not shake. The fact that I still remember my unease during this first trip into the town where we would soon live attests to its impact on my thinking at that time.

Later, I learned to appreciate that the county hospital at our destination had a special role in this region exactly because its location was so remote. Learning how traumatic injuries were managed by the medical partners serving this rural area was reassuring after I became familiar with the system. We had access to helicopter med-evac teams and small fixed wing airplanes as well, the latter being chosen when weather was more turbulent. However, the time for transport was frequently more than that first golden hour because of the distances involved. This meant that when working in our emergency department we had to provide that competent level of care that would save lives. What I did not understand until I began to practice medicine in this community was the presence of a different, more sinister danger for my patients and family.

Nearly four hours into our journey, we observed a sudden change in the color of the vegetation. The subtle browns and beiges of the native grasses along with the dull greenish gray of sage turned into vibrant green, shades of gold and deep reds of immaculately cultivated crops consisting of corn, alfalfa, sunflowers, soybeans, and grains of many varieties including sorghum and wheat. Looking for the essential ingredient, we eventually spotted irrigation canals, and in some cases, pumps connected to circular watering equipment that explained the transformation. Fields in this part of the country depend on water that is pumped from lakes below the surface known as aquifers.

We were then greeted by the odor of fresh manure from a large feedlot with thousands of fenced cattle as we approached the city limits from the west. Gradually the obnoxious smell diminished but was not eliminated as we continued towards my interview destination. Imagining this smell as a constant companion, I thought of my mother's family in Minnesota and her brothers' hog farms. My uncle had once described the odor of hog waste, even more penetrating than that of cattle, as "the smell of money." Optimistically, I imagined that I could get used to this smell of cattle penned up in feedlots.

A prominent historical marker welcomed travelers like us to a small park on the edge of Lamar and we found shade under a shelter constructed over a picnic table. Lee stopped the car and we read the display erected by

The Daughters of the American Revolution.[2] This region had been settled in the mid- to late-1800's by pioneers, among them extraordinarily strong women who were proudly identified and their stories commemorated.

Revitalized after resting and with a genuine sense of wonder as I reflected on the lives of these remarkable women, we proceeded back to the road. It brought us to a bridge where we crossed a wide but shallow riverbed with a narrow ribbon of water flowing slowly at its center. The size of the marshland and water-loving plants on both sides suggested that this river had the potential to swell and fill its banks given the right weather conditions. I would learn from the trials and tribulations of my patients in this community that the water flowing under the bridge belonged to the people of the neighboring state where it was headed. Plentiful water from the Rocky Mountains cascaded down the Arkansas River, but it was forbidden for use by the locals. Only the thirsty fields, industrial plants and population residing in the next state were allowed access to this essential moisture. This fact was hard for me to reconcile.

On the other side of the river a cavernous building appeared with a huge sign advertising its extraordinary name, *The Cow Palace*. I had never previously thought of bringing cattle into a home, much less a mansion. It looked like a gathering place, a destination for good times several decades earlier, for townspeople and perhaps tourists too. It had lost its sheen with the years that had passed. The large double entrance doors looked accessible and well-used leaving the impression that the importance of cattle to the people of this culture could not be overstated.

As is well known in American history, the struggle for control of the West during our country's past led to conflicts with unspeakable atrocities. Horrifying battles and inhumane treatment of prisoners were often women and children from the indigenous tribes or their opponents who were the immigrating population. Among the worst of these stories was the Sand Creek Massacre in 1864.[3]

The long and dangerous trek undertaken by pioneers in covered wagons, primarily after the Homestead Act of 1862, provided the path toward their personal ownership of land.[4] In the end, the expansion of settlements prevailed, and the dominant culture became that of the pioneers' origins.

2. *Madonna of the Trail*, Santa Fe Trail—Scenic and Historic Byway.

3. Hoig, *Sand Creek Massacre*, 120–76.

4. Hinz-Penner, *East of Liberal: Notes on the Land*, 121–4.

Becoming familiar with the past contributed to my understanding of the present in the region of my new home.

My job interview at the clinic apparently went well and I started this position with a great interest in learning more about my new home community. As a physician practicing in this rural location, I learned to appreciate the culture and traditions through my patients. Like every practitioner of medicine anywhere in the world, I heard a lot of interesting stories about their lives and the difficulties they faced.

Water rights disputes were often on their minds, especially at the beginning of my practice, since these farmers and ranchers felt like the deck was stacked against them. They seemed to find that sharing their daily reality with a sympathetic outsider was therapeutic. They would complain that the inhabitants next door got the water that flowed through their backyards only because their neighbors in the next state had hired better lawyers when these issues were being decided in the 1950's. The other source of water available to them should have been the aquifers but powerful competitors for this precious resource were cities springing up in the foothills of the Rockies that had rapidly growing urban populations.

The average annual precipitation for this general region was 15.9 inches according to a study undertaken between 1971–2000.[5] By the time my family and I arrived, water was already flowing to the cities from the lakes below the topsoil because many of the original homesteaders had sold their water rights. The families who were still living in this semi-arid environment had to find jobs a distance away from their homesteads to survive. Other ranchers and farmers who continued their traditional work on the land would lament to me bitterly. They wished they had affordable access to more water for their livestock and crops which would give them a better chance to make a decent living. These people were descendants of those who stayed through the Dust Bowl Era of the 1930's.[6] Hardship in these parts has been a constant, going back for generations.

Surprising to me for an agricultural community, the annual average precipitation in this river valley was so low that when it occurs and because it is so scant, rain isn't called rain. It is called moisture. Hail, sleet, and snow over the course of the four seasons every year adds to the total precipitation, a very precious commodity. Having no experience living in this arid to semi-arid climate, I had a lot to learn.

5. Currentresults.com, *Average Annual Precipitation by State*, line 6.
6. Woodard, *American Nations*, 243–53.

Chapter 2

2010-2011—A SINISTER DANGER LOOMS

I MISSED MY CHILDREN who had stayed behind when I moved with Lee to this rural Far Western community to begin my first job after residency. This was not an easy transition emotionally. My oldest son Frank was making his way in the adult world having finished his undergraduate studies in Business Administration, specializing in Marketing and Sales. He was starting his career working for an insurance company. He had a lovely girlfriend whom we adored, and I thought the distance between us might be harder on me than on him.

But Bez was a different story. He still had two more years of high school left to finish. Although I would have liked him to move with us, his dad would have none of it. Henry insisted that if I was going to move so far away, Bez should move in with him and attend a school in the community where he had started his education during elementary school. I hoped Bez would benefit from spending more time with his dad and I did my best to make my peace with this plan since this accommodating youngster was willing to give it a try.

My youngest son had cousins in the town where his father lived who were attending a private Mennonite high school and Bez wanted to be in the same environment with them. Henry and I agreed to fund this education together. I did as much as I could before leaving the area to prepare Bez for new experiences in his old hometown. I also became involved in planning his schedule of classes and met some of his teachers before his school year began. I discussed with the school administrators Bez's move into his father's and stepmother's home, which was a different environment than the home where he had lived with me for the previous six years. I explained that I was going to be far away but available for conferences and progress reports. After the school had been in session for about one month it appeared that Bez needed extra help in a couple of subjects, and I found a young tutor to work with him to provide the academic support he needed. I was disappointed that his dad couldn't be more hands-on with parenting, but I tried to stay calm, wondering how long this arrangement could continue.

I refocused my attention on my new job. Some of the physically traumatic injuries I saw that caught me off guard were related to the risks of working with large animals, specifically horses and cattle. On one of my first shifts in this out-patient clinic, a muscular young cowboy came in for an evaluation barely complaining at all as he sat straight-backed on the examination table.

I asked, "How can I help?"

He said, "I was working with cattle today, but I was not riding horseback. I got pushed into the fence during a scuffle with a steer and I fell. Next thing I remember, I was pinned to the ground when the steer stepped on my back, and I couldn't breathe. That didn't last long, luckily. I was able to get up and made it out of the pen."

Using a stethoscope, I was happy to let him know that his breathing sounded normal and reassured him by telling him his vital signs were fine.

He asked me to look at the left side of his upper back where it hurt. He removed his shirt and to my surprise there was a bright red outline of a hoof imprinted there. No break in the skin was observed but the sharp edges of the hoof had left their mark. That was something I had never seen before. I palpated the soft tissues as well as the bony structures in that area of injury and noticed he was having pain but there were no obvious signs of fracture. I ordered X-rays anyway.

Fortunately, the images confirmed there was no collapsed lung and no broken ribs, scapula, or vertebrae. His spine and the left scapula were intact which allowed the patient to return home. Surprising to me, he wasn't asking for any prescription pain medications. This toughness after a significant injury was not unusual at all as I later discovered among those from the community. Due to the scarcity of medical services in this remote location, many people I cared for avoided seeking medical attention unless there was no other way to take care of a problem. I found that the stereotypical machismo associated with cowboys relative to their ability to ignore pain, was real—a kind of fortitude I frequently observed and admired.

The avoidance of medications also seemed to be a common practice because this population was used to the aches and pain that came with a multitude of musculoskeletal injuries over a lifetime. Instead, they had been taught to use sensible home remedies, like ice for swelling, ACE bandages and elevation where it involved a damaged limb, reduced activity for a while to let healing take place and then they would gradually get back to their normal routines. Self-medicating with alcoholic beverages to treat physical and psychic pain was also a familiar source of comfort, as old a remedy as there is.

Another support during hardship was assistance from extended family and neighbors when a person was recovering from a health-related problem. No one would let cattle and horses go hungry or suffer while their owner was unable to care for them. Fields would get harvested by neighbors and the favors would be returned when their own need arose.

As in most rural agricultural communities there were also a few heavy industrial factories providing employment in this town. In fact, most of the well-paying jobs available presented a higher-than-average risk for serious debilitating work-related accidents and recovery from these injuries could require months of medical care. These injuries were more serious than what the home remedies could accommodate. One of the most concerning and vexing problems that I encountered early on was the excessive abundance of opioids prescribed for patients who had originally been treated by medical providers for acute injuries. When the initial pain did not resolve thus becoming chronic pain, many were still being prescribed opioids.

As a newly trained physician, I was looking for guidance among the medical practitioners with more experience than me. A few that I worked with were physicians, many were advanced practice providers (APP's). This group of medical providers were trained as nurse practitioners and physician assistants. After having attained a certain level of experience they were credentialed to practice medicine independently in out-patient clinics. As a result of the physician shortage everywhere, there were more APPs than physicians available to patients in this remote rural community. No matter what type of medical training we had, we were all trying to make sense of what was going on with opioid medications and the clamoring for more from our patients.

I would, at times, be asked to care for patients whose primary care provider was absent from the clinic on the day the patient needed to be seen. Unfortunately, I dreaded seeing certain patients because they requested refills of opioid medications in amounts that I was not comfortable prescribing. It wasn't that I disliked the patients. What I disliked was being the gatekeeper for drugs they had become dependent on and for whom the amounts being prescribed were not safe. What I knew from my medical training was that opioids had a risk of causing death. The higher the dosing, the higher the risk.

Whether these patients were opioid dependent for treatment of pain or truly addicted was a matter of professional opinion that was not easy for any prescriber to determine. Addiction carried with it a pattern of individuals seeking that substance even though it was causing harm. Clearly, withdrawal symptoms that also included pain were experienced by all who had to go without their daily opioid medications. Whether their pain was a result of withdrawal or related to the original injury could not be differentiated after they had become acclimated to opioids and were using them in high doses daily. However, medical practitioners all over the U.S. at that time assumed that fewer than 1 percent of patients treated with these drugs developed genuine addictions.[1]

I was not the only new physician in town who was worried about this burgeoning phenomenon in 2010 when I arrived.[2] Dr. Wayne Hudson, from the osteopathic tradition, was also opposed to liberal opioid prescribing despite assurances from the pharmaceutical sales reps we encountered at that time. Their repeated claim was that if a patient reported pain, they could safely be prescribed increasing amounts of these pills so long as they continued to take those high doses regularly. This associate of mine didn't believe any of it. His decades of experience in medicine before the new formulations of opioids appeared in the 1990's made him doubt that these so-called new formulations of opioids were safer than the previously marketed pills had been, in ever-increasing doses over long periods of time.

What was apparent was that dependence too frequently turned into addiction when patients had been prescribed any of the pharmaceutical formulations derived directly or indirectly from the opium molecule, such as hydrocodone (Vicodin, Norco), oxycodone (Percocet, Oxycontin, Roxicodone), morphine (MS Contin, Kadian, Roxanol), hydromorphone

1. Quinones, *Dreamland*, 107.

2. Fishman, *Responsible Opioid Prescribing*, 98–134.

(Dilaudid), and fentanyl (Sublimaze). This was evidenced by our patients' begging for any of these medications to which they had become accustomed. By 2012 this pleading had become deafening. Like every other community in this country, the medical providers in our town were ill-prepared to protect their patients from addiction. Unfortunately, the easy path was to give in to patients' demands. Many times, prescribers didn't even try to put up a fight because it was an exhausting and thankless task. In fact, some of the providers had themselves become dependent and were not objective about the inherent risks of prescribing opioids.

Those of us lucky enough to have had medical assistants and nurses of a similar mind about opioids would help shield us from the constant barrage of requests for these prescriptions. They were our assistant gate keepers, not a role that they should have had either.

What made it harder for us was that the medical establishment opposed our concern. Once a hospital administrator at Prowers Medical Center explained to us, a group of medical providers, that pain not treated to the satisfaction of the patient led to negative quality reviews for both the hospital and the medical provider involved. Low scores by patients could produce reduced levels of reimbursement for hospital care offered from all sources, including Medicare, Medicaid, and commercial insurance. Not wanting low scores compared with our medical peers, and not wanting our hospital to lose quality points with the regulators, professional self-preservation persuaded us to listen to this advice. The best medical providers in the country were walking a tightrope. Their livelihoods were at stake and the safety of their patients was also at risk. In the end, the pressures from many fronts on physicians, dentists and APP's caused an opioid epidemic. The pharmacists were also struggling with their responsibility regarding this dangerous situation, including the ethical and moral implications of what they were doing that was contributing to the opioid problem.

Meanwhile as a practicing physician during this frightening time, over the first few years of my work I observed a gradual reduction in the availability of prescription opioids due to overprescribing. This occurred because several of us refused to give in to prescribing practices that allowed patients to take ever increasing amounts of these drugs. Among the primary care providers, a lot of educating and updating occurred and the view that a patient could not be over-prescribed gradually changed. Part of the reason we insisted on restricting opioid medications and why we were able to change minds was that we were witnessing deaths due to accidental overdoses. Also, by reducing excessive prescribing of opioids, there was less illegal diversion to the streets of our community. Although I was initially pleased with our progress, what came next was worse, much worse. My stomach tightened into knots with an ominous premonition when I realized the problem that no one was openly talking about, neither law enforcement, local political leaders, nor medical providers.

All we could do at that time was to prescribe as carefully as possible while angering the patients by using best practices to treat their pain without increasing their risk of death by accidental overdose. We explained endlessly to our patients how they had to keep their opioids under lock-and-key at home, how they had to take only the amount prescribed on a regular schedule, and why they could not share their prescription drugs with anyone in their families or circle of friends. And of course, we told them they could not sell their medications, which was and still is strictly against the law. But we all knew it was difficult to enforce. Whenever an overdose death was announced by the authorities, we providers dreaded that there might be a prescription bottle in the vicinity with our name on it as the prescriber. That was what we had to prevent to the best of our ability. Our livelihoods were at risk because one small step over the line to make our patients happy could come back to haunt us with deadly consequences. Some, but not all of us recognized that our patients' long-term well-being and even their very lives were at stake in this deadly struggle against excessive opioid prescribing.

Chapter 3

2011–2012—BEZ MOVES TO OUR TOWN

I HAD BEEN WORKING full-time as a primary care physician for about a year when I was asked to help in the Emergency Department (ER) at our local hospital. My residency training had provided a skill set that was a good fit. Like every rural hospital ER, our team saw every type of medical situation including trauma from motor vehicle crashes, farm and industrial accidents, sepsis and other severe infections, pregnancy complications, chronic obstructive pulmonary disease exacerbations, uncontrolled diabetes and hypertension, suicidal ideation, and many other types of mental health emergencies. It was interesting and meaningful work.

When I first started working in the Emergency Department, lots of patients came in when they had run out of their pain prescription medications. That was problematic for an emergency physician for a lot of reasons that included not having any history with the patient as well as not having access to the medical record from their primary care provider's office. This lack of continuity of care was worse because we did not have access to medical records that would explain why the patient was on opioid medications. Additionally, there wasn't even a way to verify what their medical provider had prescribed or when they were last seen. Only occasionally did patients come in with an empty prescription bottle so that the dates and amounts prescribed could be verified. At that time there was no electronic prescription drug monitoring program for us to access information that we needed to prevent overprescribing. There were few supports of any kind to help us make safe decisions for the patient even when compassion would dictate that a patient should have their pain treated. Sometimes we called all the pharmacies in the area to find out what had been previously prescribed because we had no other way of knowing if there were multiple providers writing pain medication prescriptions for a particular patient. We tried to verify every patient's claim, but this extra step was only possible when the nursing staff had time to make these calls and even then, only during business hours. We tried to get as much information as we could about patients who obviously were not capable of being reliable sources given their driving desire for more opioids. We certainly tried to be responsible prescribers of these dangerous and potentially addictive drugs.

Another complicating factor for physicians was the Emergency Medical Treatment & Labor Act (EMTALA) enacted in 1986 by Congress.[1] As a result of this law, public access to emergency services was and still is mandatory regardless of ability to pay and every other type of potential assumption or bias. Thus, in the ER we could not turn away patients even when someone on the medical team was certain, due to a prior experience, that a patient was just there for the opioids. This law requires all people who present to the ER to be medically screened and stabilized. Pain is a complaint that must always be taken seriously because many illnesses begin with no other symptom. Thus, the opioid epidemic presented practical and ethical problems that were difficult for emergency physicians to navigate.

My goal was to err on the side of caution, never wanting to miss a diagnosis, and never wanting to leave a patient suffering without treating the patient compassionately. Consequently, there were times I am sure I administered opioids in the ER when they could have objectively been deemed unnecessary. But I felt my duty was to ease suffering.

What did help reduce the opioid-seeking visits after some years was the development by our hospital of an Emergency Department policy not allowing physicians to prescribe more than a 24-hour supply when the patient left the ER. We had an advantage when we could blame the hospital policy to deflect the patients' anger. It took some of the pressure off, which made it easier to do the right thing and keep the opioid prescriptions minimal.

Some patients had learned that they could not say that they came to the ER for narcotics but sometimes every other pain medication offered by the physician would be declined for a variety of reasons. Not uncommon were claims that they were allergic to *all* the other pain medications.

---

1. www.cms.gov, *Emergency Medical Treatment and Labor Act.*

Although not credible, this resulted in opioids being the only medication that we could provide for their pain.

Occasionally, patients were straightforward and came to us for help when they were in withdrawal and needed a dose or two of opioid meds for relief from their severe flu-like symptoms: extreme generalized pain, fatigue, nausea, vomiting, diarrhea, shivering, anxiety and insomnia that lasts for three to five days.[2] People who have experienced withdrawal from opioids often report that they would rather die than go through that suffering again. Remarkably, few if any medical references for medical students during that era cataloged all the symptoms of withdrawal from opioids.

Recently I looked through the textbooks I still have on my shelves that had been required when I was studying in medical school between 2001–2005. Interesting to me from my current perspective and understanding of the disease of opioid use disorder, I could not find any definitive description of opioid withdrawal in any of those books. It seems as if the medical profession had not assigned any importance to understanding the long-term effects of stopping the prescribing of a medication that we were being trained to use liberally. Consistently we were told that withdrawal never killed anyone. The inferred message was that any patient who was in withdrawal deserved their suffering because only addictive personalities and others with defective character would be afflicted with this problem.

We also saw patients who stopped at our ER as they passed through town just to test the doctor's willingness to prescribe opioids. A scarcity of these highly addictive drugs was developing all over this country and patients who were dependent and who had vehicles would travel great distances, even across state lines, to find legal sources of these prescription drugs.

At this point in the current opioid epidemic, we were starting to see complications from the use of black tar heroin. Until then, to my knowledge, the potential complications of this illegal street drug were not medically observed in our community on a regular basis. This compound was first produced commercially in 1898 by Bayer, with the chemical description, diacetylmorphine. It was named heroin.[3] When other opioids were developed by the medical researchers and pharmaceutical companies later to treat pain, heroin lost its legitimacy as a prescription drug. Since then,

---

2. Quinones, *Dreamland*, 26, 38–39, 78–79, 194.

3. Quinones, *Dreamland*, XIII.

criminal heroin producers have provided this highly addictive drug for an illegal market.

Black tar heroin is a crude form of that original legal drug but having a lot of impurities. For this reason, it is most often smoked, not injected. Even so, we observed in the ER that people could get too much and overdose. These patients sometimes arrived by ambulance and were kept alive if they were lucky. The antidote that reverses the effects of sedation when a dose is too high for the patient's tolerance is naloxone. This is the generic name of the drug now available in a nasal spray also known by its brand name Narcan.

In the ER we cared for many overdose victims who arrived unconscious and unresponsive. These patients would stop breathing altogether and suffer brain damage or death if the overdose wasn't treated quickly enough. After one dose of naloxone in the ER they would wake up within seconds, often angry and sometimes combative. To their credit, our nurses were good at quickly finding a venous site to provide that first dose of the antidote. It could also be given as an intramuscular or subcutaneous injection, but our nurses felt that the intravenous administration worked faster. We saved a lot of lives using naloxone and that was a great feeling. In those days this life-saving medication wasn't yet available in our community's ambulances so a fast trip to the ER was necessary to prevent overdose deaths.

In one particularly memorable case, a man was found by a State Trooper far from town on the side of a road in his vehicle, slumped over the steering wheel and unresponsive. This patient reportedly had a faint carotid pulse when law enforcement arrived and he was apparently breathing, but squad cars were not equipped with naloxone. As a result, the trooper could not treat the unresponsive man with the nasal Narcan spray that they now carry. Instead, he had to call an ambulance which surely took another 20 minutes or more before medical care was started. The ambulance crew rushed to bring this patient to the ER and we continued the CPR that had been initiated on scene. We gave the patient a dose of naloxone and struggled to place a line since his circulation had already ceased. His heart still had residual electrical activity, but he did not have a pulse. We attempted to resuscitate him using all means possible but the heart and brain that had been without oxygen for too long could not be revived. This unfortunate man died. I called the code to stop resuscitation efforts after a long but fruitless effort involving naloxone administration, continuous chest compressions, bagging with oxygen, intubation, accessing an artery to draw blood for labs as well as administration of medications to stimulate his heart—all to no avail.

I stood at the deceased man's bedside with the nurses and the ambulance crew, stunned by this unnecessary loss of life. As we do after witnessing a death in the ER, a minute of silence was observed as all the staff surrounding this body mourned the man's passing. He was well known to some in that room and his apparent opioid dependence was a shock to those among his rescuers who knew him.

I asked one of the volunteer EMT's quietly, "Did you try to administer naloxone on scene?"

He replied, "No, we don't have access to it in our ambulance."

In other cases when the patient arrived soon enough for us to successfully resuscitate, we would monitor them for hours, giving additional doses of naloxone since the effects of heroin or prescription opioids would last longer than the antidote we gave. Eventually the patient could be discharged.

When adequately treated, they would typically be released after a conversation with the doctor and the nurse about the importance of quitting heroin or prescription narcotics or whatever was the dangerous opioid drug of choice. Sometimes we would get a response that gave us hope that the patient understood the gravity of their situation.

The problem was that we didn't have any local programs to treat opioid use disorder and it wasn't cheap to get into rehab even when it involved going to a distant center to receive this care. Most of our unfortunate opioid-using patients didn't have the resources they needed to stop using these incredibly dangerous and addictive drugs. We also didn't have any resources in the ER to help them transition to sobriety. Incredibly, Medicaid and most commercial health insurance didn't consider opioid addiction to be an urgent life-threatening medical problem and that meant rehabilitation and detox programs were out of their reach. Patients could not get the help they needed without their own cash resources.

The unsolved problem for those caught in the web of opioid addiction was that they could not just stop using these drugs without getting professional help. An opioid user's desire to quit when the time came that they were ready to give up the drug was no match for the physical craving of the opioid molecule. In too many cases we would care for people repeatedly in the ER, literally saving their lives multiple times only to lose them to these drugs in the end. These tragedies were happening often, and they were heartbreaking and soul wrenching for all of us who were involved in their care. It surprised me at that time that there was still little public discussion about these deaths in the community. Why didn't these lives seem to matter to anyone? Where were their families and friends?

Eventually, our community leaders began talking about solving the problem. I attended a city council meeting when an officer was asked to present information about illegal drugs and how law enforcement was dealing with the local problem. During questions from the public, I asked about naloxone availability in the squad cars and in the ambulances. The Chief of Police said city officials had discussed the possibility of providing it before patients arrived in the ER but he was informed that the city's insurance cost would rise if they used this treatment as a standard of care. He said the city government had decided that they couldn't afford it. No member of the city council disagreed with this statement.

I began to ask my teenage patients how they were being educated at school regarding the risks of opioids, both for pain and for recreational use. I usually received a shrug and their parents didn't have answers either. At that time, it seemed that there was so little awareness of these drugs in the community that there was no expectation that their children should learn about this potential life-threatening risk at school.

Later, when I asked school staff, I was informed after pressing for an answer that there was no structured drug education in the curriculum. With no information on the real and present danger of drugs in their own community, teens and young adults were being seduced by drug dealers, their friends or family members who made the dangers of these drugs seem negligible. These innocent kids didn't know any better.

The other group at risk in our population were injured laborers who had become dependent on prescription opioids. To prevent withdrawal, they were forced to go out on the streets to find sources of black tar heroin, the substitute for prescription opioids when they could not get refills in the quantities they were used to. It was a terrible situation and a frightening time to be a medical provider. This remote community was not alone during this era when there were so few resources and so little awareness of the danger that lay in wait for so many.

There was so much stigma associated with heroin and other illegal drugs, people would not talk about their own family members who were struggling to recover and those with opioid use disorder were afraid to seek medical attention. The common assumption was that people who were addicted to heroin deserved what they got. It was perceived as a character flaw, a defect in training provided by the opioid user's parents or a genetically inherited trait.

My youngest son Bez has his own story about getting to know the community that became his new home when he joined us towards the end of his junior year of high school. Lee and I had moved to this rural community thinking our stay might be brief since it was so far from my two sons who continued to live in the Midwest. In addition, we were considering the well-being of both of our sets of parents who were quite elderly and needed our involvement in their lives. We had many extended family members whom we missed and a community of friends expecting us to return quite soon. However, Bez moved to live with us after the plans his dad had made for him came to an end.

My son was seventeen years old when he arrived on the Amtrak passenger train, heavily laden with bags in his arms and a pack on his back. He had always been my best little buddy, encouraging me through my many years of medical school and residency, never complaining about his lot in life as the child of a student mother. At that point I was remembering so many good times we had together as a household consisting only of mother and young son.

One memory in particular stood out. We had been together in the San Joaquin Valley for one month after Bez and I traveled to California to enable my completion of a clinical rotation in medical school while I was considering residency options. Upon our arrival, Bez was ten years old. He spent a lot of enjoyable time with Maddy and Conlin, children of our host family whose matriarch was my dear friend Jean. He made new friends his own age, went swimming every day, camped in the Sierra Nevada mountains and loved every minute of that incredible experience.

He was completely taken with the fresh lemons ripening on the trees in the backyard of the house where our generous host Gail, the daughter of Jean, had arranged for us to stay. Bez had never seen such an exotic thing in his life! These lemons were huge, perfect in appearance and the flavor of the juice was exquisite. He decided to harvest the lemons, got permission from Gail, and she watched as he set to work on his project. When I returned from work in the operating room at the hospital, I was informed that he had spent several days juicing dozens of lemons by hand. He had this wonderful idea of preserving the juice by freezing the fragrant fresh and sourly delicious liquid in ice cube trays.

When we left to return home soon afterwards, we kept the lemon juice cubes frozen in a cooler as we drove east in our sedan, allowing us to mix fresh lemonade all the way across the Sierra Nevadas, the Rocky Mountains and then halfway across the Midwest. This was a brilliant idea since ice water was available at every gas station with a convenience store. White sugar packets weren't hard to find either. We enjoyed that fresh-squeezed lemonade all the way home! What a creative and industrious child he was. Looking back, I see that he has been an original thinker and a problem solver all his life.

From a mother's perspective I was thrilled to have Bez with me again when he arrived. He had such joie de vivre and he cared about everyone around him. His friendly way of interacting was unusual and delightful with his own unique brand of humor and, yes, he was funny!

One time he had decided he should memorize some medical terms that he could throw around randomly to impress people since he was, after all, the son of a doctor. He asked me to teach him the longest medical word I could think of with the most syllables possible to be able to demonstrate the best example of complex medical terminology. At first, I was a little dubious about his motives. But in the end, I was persuaded to teach him to say with perfect pronunciation and syntax, hemophagocytic lymphohistiocytosis. Although this is a two-word phrase, not a single word, he was satisfied with the medical sophistication and worked hard to learn how to say this correctly. Of course, I made sure he was not planning to use it for any reason that might demean or be derogatory for those to whom this diagnosis is not funny. Given these strict instructions, in the right type of situation that might benefit from some levity, he would throw this 14-syllable phrase into normal conversation with a straight face and wait for the response. Hearing these words enunciated perfectly by a teenager unexpectedly in a nonmedical context, he would elicit the response desired because it was hilarious. He got a lot of mileage out of this comedy routine because his timing was perfect. He was a performer by nature and when surrounded by a group of kids his own age he was in his element.

He attended the local public high school and quickly made some wonderful friends. He seemed to be popular at school and I thought he was doing well adjusting to a different culture than what he had known previously. The local newspaper had a column featuring regional high school contributions and his essays appeared in print frequently.

Soon after Bez had first arrived in this rural town, it was time for prom.

When I first met Jodi, she was wearing a full-length formal gown made from a beautifully draping shiny fabric in a most spectacular shade of turquoise blue. It complemented her exotic darker skin and long straight black hair. She and Bez had coordinated their prom outfits so that his matched hers' perfectly, all the way from the color of her gown and wrist corsage to the vest and boutonniere that he wore on the lapel of a black tuxedo jacket. They dutifully posed for photos in our tiny back yard on this memorable occasion, absolutely delighting us with their willingness to be admired. We had no doubt that the sky was the limit when it came to their future successes in life. They made a stunning couple, and they certainly were the picture of youthful promise on that wonderful day. Like every other mother who has had to make her peace with a child growing up in front of her eyes, I had a lump in my throat and misty eyes as they headed out for the festivities.

His summer was spent working at he the locally owned drive-in restaurant. He was enjoying making some money and was saving up for his college expenses. He got to know the families of his school friends who enjoyed him, and he learned a lot about Mexican foods and also learned some Spanish in the homes of his friends. He was getting to know a lot of the neighbors in his age group.

During his final year in high school, he was enrolled in an advanced course called Health and Wellness. He and his classmates were given an assignment to work together on a project of their own design that they were told would be presented to their peers. The topic they chose was "How and Why to Avoid Teen Pregnancy." Bez was doubtless aware of the difficult decisions his birth mother had to make when she was pregnant and had decided to place him for adoption at birth. As a result, he had more sensitivity than most kids his age regarding the difficult choices that would be inevitable when a teenager became pregnant. He had told me as a newcomer in this community that he was surprised by the number of girls in school who were obviously pregnant. He thought it might be useful to educate all the students at his high school about the advantages of avoiding pregnancy during the teen years. The school nurse told me at the time that Bez was an amazing advocate for the education of his peer group, and he had many ideas that were used in the video that was produced. I had also heard good reports from several adult leaders of the significant efforts of this class and the leadership that Bez provided at that time.

Towards the end of his senior year in high school he was selected by the Class of 2012 to emcee their group presentation for parents and community members in a demonstration of the skills and talents they had developed over the years as students in this school district. He delivered his lines with confidence and a natural ability to speak to a large audience. He was tall at six feet, with a lean build, long legs, and perfectly beautiful hands with long, slender fingers. His natural dark brown curls were stylish in a conservative cut, his brown eyes were highlighted with prominent dark eyebrows and high cheekbones decorated with a sprinkling of freckles. A biased and proud mother could probably be forgiven for realizing that her son was becoming a handsome young man.

The next day as we walked together in the town's grocery store, one of his teachers caught up with us and said, "Good job up there last night, Bez. You were fantastic!"

Nonetheless, he seemed so unimpressed by his success, taking it all in stride. I was sure I could not have delivered a performance equal to his if I had been in his place. He had gifts and talents to share with the world, no question.

The weekend of Bez's graduation from high school was a big family event. Frankie had brought his sweetheart to celebrate this milestone with us. Adding to our joy, they became engaged to be married when Frank stopped their rental car in a public park surrounded by the incredible beauty of red rock formations in the foothills of the Rocky Mountains under a cloudless blue sky. He had deliberately taken a detour to the Garden of the Gods on the drive from Denver with the intention of surprising her with his proposal. Since she had gotten on the flight with him after finishing a night shift as an ER nurse in Chicago, she was drowsy and a little disoriented when she awoke to Frank's insistence that they take a walk to enjoy the beauty surrounding them. After she had fully awakened and was able to appreciate this astonishing environment, he dropped on one knee and presented his surprised girlfriend with a diamond ring. Other tourists were enjoying the scene when he popped the big question, to which she responded, "Yes!"

Bez hugely enjoyed having them join us for this celebratory weekend. These brothers still had a close bond. Two of my friends from other parts of the country also participated in the festivities in our remote community that weekend. Even Bez's octogenarian grandparents made the trip for the occasion.

Since we were relatively new in town and still lived in an apartment with only a postage-stamp-sized backyard, I had asked around but had not been able to locate a venue to rent for Bez's graduation party. My incredibly sweet and capable medical assistant from the clinic, Denise Quintana, offered us the use of her home with its large lawn, almost unheard of in these parts. She even offered to cook for the event and a memorable buffet appeared like magic with all of Bez's favorite Mexican delicacies!

It was a wonderful gathering of friends and family, and everyone had a great time. Bez had many school friends who stopped in, and this gave me a chance to meet some of his classmates whom I had not yet encountered in person. Lots of special photos were taken to memorialize the events surrounding this milestone. It was a truly fabulous family weekend, and a lot of lifelong memories were made over the course of those few days.

Chapter 4

2012–2013—AND HE'S OFF
TO COMMUNITY COLLEGE

ON THE SURFACE ALL was well. I was constantly evaluating my career plans, trying to decide when it would make sense to return to the Midwest where I had originally planned to live and work. Thinking that the success of Bez's graduation from high school would provide a foundation that would continue to support him in life I began to relax my thoughts about relocating.

At that pivotal point in Bez's life, Lee and I were discussing with him what he would be doing next. My husband thought that it would be wisest for our new high school graduate to stay in the town where we were living to attend junior college for the first two years, but Bez had his heart set on enrolling in a state university that was two hours away. He and a friend had already looked at that campus together and decided this is where they would both enroll in fall. They were both accepted, and Bez was excited about his future. I was impressed by his initiative and thought it might be a good idea to let him get his higher education started where he had already made a commitment. The only factor that was holding me back from supporting his plan was my concern about some impulsive inclinations that could spell danger for him if he was too far from home.

FIRST INTRODUCTION TO ALCOHOL

There was a time when our family had gone back to visit extended family. While there, Bez had been visiting a friend from high school days who took him to a party where he was apparently offered shots of hard liquor. He drank too many of those and ended up blacking out.

The fact that Bez could not or would not choose to stop drinking shots after he had gotten started was a revelation of significance to me and very frightening to us as his parents. What exactly did this mean? Was it impulsiveness that caused the poor decision? Was it ignorance of the danger of too much alcohol that caused this? Were there other dynamics at the party to blame? Who were these supposed friends and why did they allow him to drink so many shots? And, importantly, who supplied the alcohol? These kids were minors and should not have been attending that party in the first place. Did Bez have an undiagnosed mental health issue?

I asked Bez later, "What were you thinking when you decided to drink those shots?"

He replied, "I wanted to know what it would feel like to drink until I got drunk. I haven't ever had this experience and I just wanted to know what it was like."

Then, "Why did you want to get drunk?"

"I don't know," was his reply.

Lee and I talked at length about the decision regarding Bez's plans for college. Not understanding why Bez wanted to leave our town so badly, I ended up agreeing with Lee that he should stay in our community and take the first two years at the local community college. We thought he would transfer to the university two years later. It seemed to me that if he could wait until he had a couple more years of maturity and life experiences, he would be better prepared to function well and maintain his life without having us close by. When I began to understand the changes that happened in my son's life after his closest friends from his graduating class left him behind, it wasn't as clear that he had advantages in staying close to us.

STRANGER IN A STRANGE LAND

Some of Bez's high school friends were from the original homesteading families who had strong connections to their families' ranches and farms. Many of them had plans to return to their families' land after leaving the area temporarily to attend college or trade schools. Their dreams included plans to return to the area to marry someone from their town and raise their own children someday.

Other friends of his who came from families who were hired hands in the feedlots or laborers in metal fabrication, ranches, farms, or the hospitality industries, didn't have land ownership built into their futures. Hispanic cultural values were different from those of the dominant culture.[1] In addition to their on-going financial limitations as well as a cultural expectation that they would get laboring jobs after high school to help support their families of origin, higher education was not usually considered an option.

Like other cultures everywhere in the world during the transition between childhood and adulthood, these teens' future lives were already outlined for them. This included who they could spend time with, who was in their circle of trusted family and friends, and who could be invited to join their social circle. Strangers to the community, like us, would be unlikely to be genuinely accepted by either culture, no matter how long we stayed. This was not immediately obvious to me.

Since I had never lived in a remote Far Western community, I was interested in the cultures that surrounded us. I wanted to understand what it was that determined community priorities and how decisions were made to run the schools, to run city and county governments and to negotiate with the state government to obtain their fair share of available resources.

Bez had his own ruminations regarding fitting in with the people in this community. He had to accommodate the additional layer of two new cultures rivaling the two that he had already learned about as a child in our family.[2] Sometimes the love of a mother and father is not enough to provide all the protection and support that a child needs.

His stepdad and I had been fortunate to be able to help Bez move into the apartment next door when he started his first year at the junior college. He had been an energetic painter and decorator when we rented the unit for him, and he found a friend to move in with him to share the expenses. He already had some earnings saved from his after-school job at the drive-in down the street. He spent it on furniture for his new apartment. He bought a brand-new couch and loveseat that looked sharp in the new décor of the apartment. For his birthday, he asked for a large dining room table and several chairs that he had spotted at the resale shop on Main Street. He had replaced the old dining room's light fixture with a new one that provided style as well as improved light. Now the dining room table and chairs made

1. Woodard, *American Nations*, 23–33.
2. Woodard, *American Nations*, 92–111.

a great surface for studying and eating. It was easy for us to move things next door that Bez and his roommate needed in the kitchen. I also bought him a desktop computer as a graduation gift for his assignments at school.

TRYING TO FIT IN

One additional personal issue Bezzy also had to figure out was whether he was going to continue taking the Ritalin that had helped him in high school. During his senior year he began resisting taking it. I asked him what it was that made him uncomfortable taking this prescribed drug.

After pressing him repeatedly since he was refusing to take Ritalin, he told me, "My friends tell me I am different when I am taking it. They don't like the person I become. They say I am not friendly, I act kinda' mean and they don't like me."

Bez is a people-loving person and this feedback from his peers was difficult for him. He insisted that he didn't need it to succeed in school and he stopped taking the medication for ADHD. Nevertheless, he got through his first year at the community college successfully. He had passed most if not all of his classes and planned to enroll for a second and final year to complete his associate's degree before transferring to the four-year university.

As planned, Bez's brother Frank got married at the end of the next summer near Chicago. When Bezzy returned to our home after spending a week there with a family friend while his brother and new sister-in-law were on their honeymoon, he tells me now that he was incredibly depressed. Upon his return, anticipating starting his second year at the junior college where he did not want to be, he has admitted retaliating at least a little against the decision we made to keep him close to us. He said yes to a question posed by one of his friends that led him down a path that would ultimately be the worst decision of his young life.

Chapter 5

2013-2014—THE NIGHTMARE OF HEROIN

WHEN BEZ GOT OFF the train after dog and apartment sitting during his brother's honeymoon, he was picked up by friends in our town with whom he had been talking on the phone all week, anticipating his return. He phoned me before the train came into the station and told me not to meet him.

He said, "I already have a ride. My friends are picking me up."

I asked, "Why are your friends picking you up?"

"They are so excited that I am back," he replied.

Bez didn't come home right away after I heard the train whistle while leaving the station and I was surprised. I thought he would come bouncing into our apartment to tell me all about his adventures in Chicago. I was becoming worried after a couple of hours. When he did arrive his eye lids looked very heavy and after I remarked about it he said he hadn't gotten any sleep on the overnight train. It seemed plausible and I wanted to believe him. He didn't look right but there weren't any other signs of drugs or alcohol from what I could see or smell. I hoped it wasn't something like that, but I was concerned because he seemed defensive and a little edgy with me. He wasn't the happy kid I expected to see that day.

So began his second year at the local community college.

He had decided against keeping his apartment over the summer months and was looking for a new arrangement to live off-campus. There weren't enough dorms at his community college for all the students so those who had family locally were expected to provide their own room and board.

I realized he wanted a little more distance from us than he had during his first year of college. The trouble was that there were not many places to live. He ended up moving into a small, older, ranch-style house that had been rented by some students at the college and it was on the edge of town. These kids threw some parties, and they had good times together from what I heard. Bez invited me there several times to see how they had arranged their furniture and their other assets for the benefit of all three occupants. He was so proud to be able to share what he had with them. His rectangular solid pine dining room table was very well suited for the large old-fashioned kitchen. He told me it was the pride of the household that they could fit so many in there when they had parties.

After one of these gatherings, the house was not occupied for some hours while these kids were all at school. Bez returned home to find his computer missing. Bez was distraught. I was upset. Since his window had been pried open to gain access to the computer, I became worried about his safety at that location. They called the police, but the thief was not apprehended; the computer was gone for good. If I remember correctly, their landlord got wind of the parties and the break-in with the police being called and he threw them all out immediately. Bez's roommates were from a distant community, so they had access to the dorms. Bez needed a different place to live. Our apartment complex had a vacant unit available, so he moved across the courtyard with our help.

Bez was, by then, struggling academically and he was physically and emotionally keeping his distance from us. He wasn't giving me much information and since he was now legally an adult, I wasn't getting any reports from his teachers. Although I knew he was now old enough to make daily decisions, I didn't know what was going on in his head. When he came home for dinner which was rare, I remember a couple of times sitting across the table from Bez when Lee tapped my leg with his foot, then leading me with his eyes to Bez's face alerting me to what he was noticing. Bez's lids were so heavy it appeared that he could hardly keep his eyes open. It wasn't normal sleepiness either. Something was wrong, and Bez wasn't admitting anything when I tried to talk to him about this. Wow. What is a mother to do? I felt sure that a disaster was coming but I was paralyzed by uncertainty, and I didn't want to lose his trust.

During the second semester of his second year at the community college, Bez's dad decided to invite him along on a trip to the Philippines. I objected since Bezzy would still be in school and I knew that the interruption would further affect his performance. Bez really wanted to go. His dad and I vehemently disagreed with each other, but Bez chose to take the trip. I had been telling his dad that something was amiss and that I was concerned about drug use. Perhaps Henry thought he could figure out Bez's problem if he spent a couple of weeks with his son? I didn't know why he was so sure that the trip was a wise decision.

When Bez returned after his two weeks away from school, he was very happy about the trip but he was in a lot of trouble with his teachers. Adding to the downward spiral, Henry decided upon returning home that he would check the balance in the savings account he still maintained for Bez's higher education. What he found is that Bez had been withdrawing money regularly for seven months. There had been almost $20,000 at the beginning of the school year and now there wasn't much left. The good news was that this wasn't illegal because Bez had his name on the account. The bad news was that he had been lying to me and Lee after all. In addition, Henry never suspected that Bez would be accessing money without discussing it with him despite my expressed concerns about possible drug use. Since Lee and I had been paying all Bezzy's school fees, I knew the money wasn't being used for that purpose.

This discovery was a shock for his dad and for me and Lee as well. I confronted Bez. He made excuse after excuse, none of which made any sense. I knew they were lies; all lies. Bez promised this would stop and he said he planned to repay the account. I didn't want to believe he was using heroin but the amount of money he had run through in a few months forced me to recognize the likelihood that this was the truth. In addition, his symptoms were consistent with the use of an opioid. I had been seeing heroin overdoses in the ER and by then I knew black tar had become easily available in this community. Where were his track marks? How was he using this drug?

Very concerned now, I started to monitor his activities more closely. I had a key to his apartment and knocked on his door late one morning. He didn't answer. It was completely quiet on the other side. His Chevy, a hand-me-down from Lee, was parked in the street in front of his apartment as usual. I took out my key and unlocked the door.

I hollered out to him when I entered, "Bezzy!"

Silence.

"Bez, are you here?"

But there was no reply. My heartbeat loud and rapid in my chest, I started walking through the large, mostly unfurnished space. Oh my God, was he dead? Fearing the worst, I started walking faster through the apartment. First, in the basement there were several large rooms that were not completely finished. No one there. I moved up to the main floor and looked in the kitchen which was a mess with garbage and aluminum foil everywhere. There were large bags of undisposed garbage that hadn't been taken out to the dumpster and it didn't smell too good. I didn't stay long. I walked into the living and dining room area. There was a large TV, the one we had purchased as a Christmas gift a while back. No one there. I walked up the stairs to the next floor and peaked into one of the two bedrooms up there.

I was startled when I found Bez asleep on the floor. There was no bedframe, no mattress, just a couple of sleeping bags with him lying on top of them and a blanket covering him. His chest was rising and falling regularly but his face looked white as a ghost. I looked around to find that the floor of his bedroom was covered with clothing and other miscellaneous items including textbooks and binders. There was no furniture in there. This was not the way my artistic, creative kid liked to live. My heart sank and I tried not to panic.

Kneeling next to him I said softly, "Bez, wake up."

He didn't stir.

His skin was paler than I had ever seen it and that worried me. Watching him, I could see that his chest was still rising and falling so I knew he was breathing. I moved closer and talked to him quietly at first and then touched his shoulder. Not getting any response I shook it gently. He opened his eyes and slowly began to focus them on me. He wasn't happy to see me.

"Why did you wake me up?"

"I just came to see you. It is almost noon. Remember, you told me to stop by anytime."

He shook his head and mumbled, "Not now, okay?" and immediately went back to sleep.

I let myself out of the apartment. I didn't know what to do at that point. I pondered. I talked about this with Lee. He and I were at odds and couldn't figure out what to do next.

The breaking point came soon after that when Bez's TV was stolen from his apartment. He called me because he was so indignant and probably because he felt he needed me to be an advocate for him. He was furious.

This was the second time since he had moved out on his own that one of his valuables had been stolen and he was really, really mad.

Bez called the police to report it. I got there before the police arrived. The police officer who came to his apartment was polite and asked to see where the television had been located. Bez invited him into his apartment.

I watched and listened to Bez as he talked with the officer.

The officer asked him, "Why would someone want to steal from you?"

"I don't know. The only thing I know is that there are people who were aware that I was going to the lake today. When I got home after being out all day, the TV was gone."

"How did they get in?" Bez showed the officer the window that had been pried open. While he spoke with Bez there was a detective who arrived and started walking around the apartment looking at everything.

I followed the detective, mystified about the whole situation. It was anything but a routine complaint of theft. I was thankful that the officers were kind and respectful towards Bez who was upset. I was acquainted with these police officers since we often had to work together in the emergency department to help people in distress; we had managed a huge variety of situations together already. Never had I been in a situation like this where my own family was involved with the police. Yes, he was the victim of theft but why the police were so interested in his apartment was a clue to me that they knew something that I didn't. I dreaded learning the truth about what Bez was caught up in.

It was necessary for me to listen carefully to these officers because at that point I didn't know what to do to help my own son. There I was, a physician, and completely in the dark about next steps for a situation that had yet to be revealed to me. I couldn't help Bez until he was willing to tell me the truth.

I was scared and shaken. My husband was not there with me. I had noticed that Lee always did his best to avoid being connected with potential embarrassment and difficulties that he felt were not his responsibility. The parental role was left to me alone whenever the going got rough. I tried to understand but I was feeling abandoned.

Bez's apartment was a mess which was not like him. He was, by nature, well organized and he cared a lot about how things looked. The kitchen was a large room with a lot of counter space, most of which was covered with empty cardboard pizza containers and empty 2-liter plastic pop bottles. There were large sized heavy-duty garbage bags sitting on the floor in the corner of this room, filled with refuse including some food waste. Just like the last time I was in here it didn't smell too good, and I was not pleased to see the condition of his kitchen. This is not how he was raised.

I opened a cabinet and found pieces of aluminum foil that had narrow black stripes running along one side of the foil. Each of the blackish brown one-quarter inch wide stripes was about 12 inches long. These sheets of foil had been neatly stacked up on the shelves, one on top of the other. I was holding one of those trying to understand what it was when the detective arrived in the room and explained that this was the residue left by black tar heroin that had been burned and inhaled. I listened and tried to take it in. I was puzzled why Bez would be inviting officers into his apartment if he had left such clear evidence of heroin use in the cabinets of his kitchen? Was this really what it was? I didn't want to believe this was true. A wave of disbelief washed over me and I felt like I might faint. I steadied myself by holding onto the countertop. The detective was watching me and I was trying to be brave. Breathe, just breathe. No questions. I couldn't let on how much I didn't know.

The detective and I walked toward the living room where the apartment complex manager had joined the conversation between Bez and the officer. This manager lived in the unit next to Bezzy and he had a right to be curious about the visit from the police since the security of the apartments was his responsibility.

The first thing I heard him say in a loud voice was, "How could you have let people know you were going to be gone all day? The people you are hanging out with are not trustworthy. You should be protecting your valuable things with your life!"

Bez looked at him and then looked away, walking towards the front door. We all followed him outside.

The detective was standing on the step outside Bez's front door when he offered an opinion to the assembled group while addressing me. "I think your son is probably a runner for drug dealers."

Bez jumped in and vehemently disagreed. "No, that is not true! I give rides to friends and classmates from school because they don't have cars and there is no bus, taxi, or Uber in this town. It isn't that easy to lug groceries and other big items around without a vehicle!"

With emphasis Bez said again, "I would never deal drugs or help drug dealers."

The detective patiently addressed me a second time. "Your son might not know that he is helping the drug dealers by giving all these people rides."

At that point the apartment manager, now angry, turned to Bez. "My kids live next door and I have seen people come in here that I know are using drugs."

The manager added, "I have even seen used syringes outside on the ground next to this apartment! These are from your so-called friends when they come to visit you."

These accusations were very upsetting to Bez who immediately proclaimed, "I don't know anyone who is using needles. I would not be spending time with people who are using IV drugs."

Writing about this terrible situation after all these years, I must stop and take a breather. This memory is so dissonant, I cannot continue. Tears fill my eyes and my intense emotional response makes me realize that this is very hard for me to share. It is a personal story, but it is not unlike that of many others living close to family members struggling with this disease.

I retreat to a quiet corner where I like to read in my home to work through the complexity of these feelings. I select a book of poetry written by my treasured friend Jean Janzen. Finding the poem she had written for her grandson Nyeland about a time when she could hold and comfort him, its reading transports me to a beautiful place.[1]

CHILD DIVING

> He points his small body,
> arms out for the arc,
>
> and holds his breath for the plunge,
> the rise. Again and again
>
> he breaks into the mirrored sky.
> This time, in reckless joy,
>
> he nicks his head against
> the flagstone edge and rises
>
> among the spreading stain.
> I hold him then; he shivers
>
> against my heat. I press
> against his blood's release

1. Janzen, *Piano in the Vineyard*, 54.

until the doctor, with curved
needle, joins the jagged gash,

what we later love to touch
in its mending, the way we love

the ecstasy of falling, although
imperfectly into a perfect sky,

loving even its borders- -
a place to fall and to be held.

At the time of this frightening episode, I had no assurance that my son could survive and recover from opioid use disorder. The shocking impact of this encounter with the landlord and the police in Bezzy's apartment has never faded but the beauty of the words of the poem I had just read soothed my mind and gently stroked my aching heart. The poem had reminded me that all of us as children, diving and falling at any age, still need to be comforted.

As I have grown older, I have discovered that when prayers are not enough, poetry brings the human experiences of others to where I am in my suffering. The writer I had chosen to read on this occasion was from my culture of origin who by the telling of her own story in verse touched me as I remembered the intensity of my pain.

I then began understanding my need to forgive Lee who had been absent at a time when I wanted his comforting presence. Love made forgiveness possible after all these years. Perhaps his own fear, ambivalence, or anger towards our son, had prevented him from grasping how much I needed him to be at my side. I could forgive him now after I was able to admit, so many years later, that we are all frail. I could now put myself in his shoes and understand. I realized that while protecting ourselves we fail to reach out to connect meaningfully with persons in our lives who desperately need us. Forgiving him helped me continue the difficult task I had undertaken. I went back to my desk to continue writing.

The landlord said emphatically, "I am going to have to evict your son."

This man was large and muscular, deliberately intimidating Bez by standing too close to him. Mentally, I debated what I could do to defuse the tension. Without having many options, I moved between them to protect my son as well as to prevent an impulsive blow by the landlord in front of the police officers that I was sure he would regret. If I was shaken before, I was now trembling like the leaves of an aspen tree.

Authoritatively, I stood as tall as I could and said loudly so that my voice would not quaver, "I will take care of this."

The threat of violence dissipated and everyone including the police officer and detective left the doorstep of Bez's apartment. I took a breath of relief, happy that no blows were exchanged and that my son was, at least for the moment, safe. But what was next? Clearly, he had to vacate the apartment. Where could he go?

It took Lee several days to get the apartment cleaned out. My husband's love for me was demonstrated in this pragmatic expression. Bez was hardly around at all, but we were paying the rent, and we had the responsibility to get him out of there. I was working so many hours at the clinic that I couldn't help much with the cleanup effort. There I was, abandoning my uncomplaining husband while he took care of the mess! Nevertheless, with Lee's steady work Bez's things were moved, the garbage had been dumped and the apartment was clean enough to vacate. Like the earlier theft of the desk top computer, Bezzy's television was not ever found by the police and returned to him.

Bez had always been a popular kid and he was still in contact with his friends from our previous home in the state where we lived during my medical residency. Not long after that doorstep confrontation Bez persuaded a friend to get on the train and meet him in the town where we lived. They then packed up his little Chevy and headed back to the Midwest together. After they left, I didn't hear from him very often even though I kept my phone next to my bed every night so that I wouldn't miss a call if it came. During the time that I wasn't working I was thinking non-stop about Bez and trying to figure out how I could reach him emotionally so that he would tell me what he was doing. Otherwise, I didn't know how I could help, and I feared that one of these days he would be gone from me forever.

I made a special trip to visit Bez before Christmas to meet a family that had befriended him and was providing him a place to stay. They were kind people, and I was thankful that he had a safe place to put his head on a pillow at night. The grandmother who was his host in that household invited me to come for dinner. We ate the delicious homemade meal she had prepared, all seated around the dining room table. I felt that this family's hospitality was genuine. Bez admitted to me that he was not working. Since I was not supporting him financially, I wondered how long this generous grandmother would be able to continue taking care of my son who should be paying his own way. He said he was still looking for a job.

After we had finished eating Bez asked me for some cash so that he could put some gasoline in his car. He and his friend promised to return within minutes. I tried to keep the conversation going with the family while we watched TV in the living room waiting for their return.

After a while, in the kitchen, the grandmother said, "Doesn't it seem odd that your son and my grandson took off after you gave them some cash and that they have been gone for so long?"

I admitted to her that it wasn't normal, that's for sure. The grandmother would not speculate further, and we left it at that. There we were, loving these young people and both of us at a complete loss as to what to do next. After about an hour they finally returned, and I prepared to say good-bye.

Before leaving I tried to talk to Bez but didn't get anywhere since he was avoiding any conversation of a serious nature. It was late and time to go. I thanked the generous grandmother, and we exchanged phone numbers. I asked her to give me a call if she needed to reach me for any reason.

Although the hostess hadn't asked me for money, after this visit I did receive a phone call from her daughter. I understood this caller was the mother of my son's friend. She told me that Bez and her son had taken a lot of money from the grandmother's back account. Somehow the account had been accessed without her permission and more than eight-hundred dollars was missing. I had no way of knowing if this was true and I couldn't reach Bez on the phone to ask him about this accusation. Since I knew he had a debt to this family I felt obligated to pay what the daughter asked of me. It was not my duty, but I knew that Bez was alive because there were compassionate people out there who were keeping him fed and warm. Winter was coming and I wanted Bez to have a chance to live long enough to recover.

After I had returned home one night when I had barely gotten to sleep, the phone rang. It was the young man who had befriended Bez in the town where he had started high school and whose grandmother had provided him with a place to stay.

He said, "I am calling because I think Bez is going to commit suicide."

I sat straight up, listening carefully. This friend of my son's told me that he and Bez were shooting up and that Bez was using doses so high that this friend was convinced that without intervention he would overdose and die.

This was the phone call that I had dreaded but had expected for so long. Shocked at first, then terrified with my heart in my throat I thanked him for calling me and then asked if I could talk to Bez?

"Yes, he is right here. You can talk to him."

At that point, Bez did admit to me for the first time that he was using heroin. He said, "I hate my life."

I asked him if he was ready to quit and go into a rehab program?

"Yes," His voice sounded strained and quiet.

I quickly made a mental calculation of what the possibilities were for him, still living so far from me. Knowing that I might not get another chance to speak with him, I quickly came up with a plan to which he agreed. Since Henry lived only two hours away, Bez agreed to move in with him and his stepmother if they would agree.

I explained to Bez, "I need to arrange to get off work long enough to come to where you are."

I asked him if he was going to be able to stay safe until I could arrive. I told him I could come immediately. He told me it would be enough to know that I was working on a plan for his rehab that would keep him motivated to stay sober. I wondered how he could stay sober without detox and rehab, but I was trying to trust him.

He would go into rehab after I had found a program that would be appropriate for his needs. I didn't know how long that would take. Bez was covered under my health insurance plan as a dependent and I would need to figure out how to get him into one of those programs.

As it turned out, it was about six weeks before I was able to travel to where he was to bring him back with me. During the intervening time I spoke on the phone with Bez often and he assured me that he was doing fine and not using heroin. I didn't believe him, truthfully, but his mood was much better, and he said he was happy to be back in his old town. I told his dad that he was probably using heroin, but Henry said he didn't believe me. His dad and stepmother had, however, taken Bez in and they were providing him with food and shelter while they waited for my arrival. Bezzy was not expressing thoughts of depression or self-harm at that time, and I felt safe in delaying my trip to bring him back to my home in Colorado.

I had planned to fly back to the Midwest for the birth of my first grandchild. Since this would occur near the location where his dad lived, Bez reassured me that the delay was going to work out just fine. He said there was no hurry for me to come sooner. I took him at his word because it was important to me to be there with Frank and his wife during the arrival of their first child, our first grandchild.

Bez knew that the birth of this baby was going to be another huge family event and he was also excited about becoming an uncle. Getting away from work was not easy for me so there was this juggling act I was trying to perform to keep all the balls in the air. Bez understood. He was always like that. His needs would wait until the others who also needed me had gotten the attention they wanted and deserved. I prayed that Bez would be safe until I got there.

Chapter 6

2015—FINDING TREATMENT
FOR OPIOID USE DISORDER

When I picked up Bez from his dad's, I was excited about the imminent birth of our first grandchild. The day before my daughter-in-law went into labor, I had been lucky to have lunch with her and we were able to visit peacefully before the birth process began. Frankie called me the next afternoon to let me know that contractions were underway so it might be good to head over to their community's hospital in a few hours.

Bez and I had time to go to a movie first, which was a good distraction while we waited for the time to pass. His was a calm presence, and I was loving the precious time I had with him while we enjoyed a movie together, reminiscent of old times.

I was shivering in the chilly winter night when we later headed west towards Lake Michigan, directly into the snow squall that came off that large body of water. Not particularly enjoying the driving conditions I was happy that Bez was accompanying me. He was animated and good company for me, providing a good selection of upbeat music as I drove.

We met my daughter-in-law's family on arrival. They were already in the waiting room of the obstetrics unit at the hospital. That we made it safely in the blowing snow was a gift that night. That my wonderful daughter-in-law delivered a stunningly beautiful and healthy baby girl that night was the greatest gift of all. Seeing this newborn baby for the first time through the glass window of the newborn nursery and realizing that she was my granddaughter gave me just indescribable joy! Bez was there too, thrilled about his new role as an uncle and so amazed by the tiny new person joining our family.

A few days later it was time for me to return to my job. Bez had parked his trusty Chevy at his grandparents' house and before we left to get on our flight, I had asked Frank to oversee the car's safe storage. I had not taken the time to look at the Chevy's interior. What I was told later by the new father, is that when he had a friend pick it up as a favor to park it in his own driveway in a different town, there was IV drug paraphernalia in the vehicle. This was disturbing to say the least! Frankie took the car to get it cleaned because he was pretty grossed out and worried. He was informed after the detailing shop started the project that there would be an extra charge if they were going to be persuaded to not call the police. My daughter-in-law, the new mother, of course heard about this potentially legally compromising situation and was understandably angry and extremely upset. This all happened after I had left the area, and I was horrified by what I had unwittingly asked them to do.

Meanwhile, Bez and I had started our journey back home. Driving to the airport together, Bezzy was surprisingly grumpy. As the time passed during our two-hour drive, he became more and more irritable.

He wanted me to stop at one of the gas station convenience stores, and not understanding the urgency I asked, "Why?"

Bez said, "There is a particular brand of sausage sandwich that they sell at this store that I want to have once more before I leave the area."

Instead, I kept going because I was concerned about the limited time we had before our flight started boarding. At that point he became verbally abusive. He was literally screaming at me by the time we got to the airport. This behavior was so crazily unlike Bez that I quickly parked the rented car, grabbed my luggage, and dashed to follow him into the terminal. After checking in for our flight, Bez walked quickly towards the TSA security line. I knew he was terribly aggravated, and he seemed to be trying to distance himself from me. He is tall and he has long legs that allow him to move a lot faster than me. We had flown out of this airport many, many times and I knew he could find his way to our gate without my help, but I wanted to know where he was going. I ran to keep up.

I saw him hurry into the men's bathroom that was located next to the security line. It was a large facility with multiple stalls, likely a mirror image of the women's room next to it. Although hoping to make a visit myself to the women's restroom after our long drive, I didn't because I was worried that I would miss him coming out of the men's restroom.

I looked at my watch and sat down. I had been waiting for five minutes when I started calculating how much time we had before we would miss our flight. I watched many men go in and come out of that restroom. I started to wonder if I should go into the men's room myself and find out if he was okay. I thought about calling airport personnel to ask for help. I was starting to sweat and realized that something was terribly wrong. Just as I prepared to walk into the men's restroom to call out to him, he appeared.

His face was completely changed. He had become calm but so much so that he appeared sedated. His eyelids seemed too heavy for him to keep them open; he looked sleepy. He walked at a normal pace and seemed surprised to see me sitting on the bench outside the men's room. He smiled at me, nodded, and kept walking toward the TSA security line, staying ahead of me. By this time the line of passengers waiting for clearance was even longer than before and I was not sure we were going to make it before our gate closed for boarding. Bez kept going as he followed the line to the TSA checkpoint.

I held my breath, afraid. What would happen if he was identified as drug-intoxicated and what if he was prevented from getting on the plane? I had never been in a position of wondering about these things before. I had no idea of what the possibilities were. Mostly, I was worried that Bez would not make it to Colorado alive. What if he overdosed and succumbed on the plane? I didn't know what to do. My lack of practical street knowledge about opioid addiction and how to care for him as a parent was very frightening.

I didn't know then that I should have had a pre-loaded syringe with naloxone in my purse to reverse a potential heroin overdose. Narcan intranasal spray, now so easily used by anyone observing an overdose, was not available at that time. Apparently, I wasn't thinking clearly about what I didn't want to admit. This son of mine needed to have friends and family members that were trained and prepared to save his life!

Boy, talk about sheltered. I knew what to do in an emergency room to save a patient who had overdosed but I was unprepared to save my own son's life on the street or in an airplane. It makes me shudder now to think about how close we came to disaster.

I had a lot to learn, I realized then. My lack of preparation was at least in part a result of the fact that I didn't know where to go for the information I needed. I had been trying to use my medical sources and I wasn't finding any information for people like me who just wanted to know how to prevent overdose deaths in their own families. There was so much negativity surrounding this subject that few, like me at that time, had enough strength to paddle upstream to get the answers we needed.

Bez boarded the plane ahead of me. It was a small jet, only three seats wide. When I got on board the aircraft, I spotted him already seated across the narrow aisle and about two rows behind me. Typical of his gregarious personality, he had started a friendly conversation with the young woman seated next to him. I was hugely relieved, seeing that he appeared to be functioning normally. After smiling at him and letting him know I had seen where he was located, I turned around then very deliberately and looked straight ahead, focusing my efforts on trying to look unconcerned. After about five or ten minutes the flight attendant who had been chatting with me since my arrival in the front row said with some alarm in her voice, "That passenger looks drugged."

Following her gaze, I turned around and saw that she was referring to Bez, who was asleep with his mouth hanging open, lips parted, his body completely flaccid. As a physician I checked for signs of hypoxia or evidence of respiratory failure from where I was seated. I saw none of these alarming signs. His lips were not blue and his skin was still pink so he must be breathing.

I responded to the flight attendant, "That is my son. He is okay."

As a physician, I am accustomed to being the one who is reassuring my team to prevent unnecessary panic. I couldn't get up to check on him more closely because the pilot and flight crew were preparing for take-off. I kept repeating to myself that Bez was breathing so he was going to be okay.

The flight attendant changed the subject. At that point I had very nearly stopped breathing myself and I tried very hard not to show that I was worried. I tried to be unobtrusive as I glanced repeatedly at the flight attendant because I knew she was watching my son from where she was seated with her back to the cockpit. After lift-off when another 15 minutes had passed, I casually turned around and saw that Bez had picked up his conversation with his seatmate, now awake. He was looking like himself. I could breathe again. Oh man, how much more would I have to witness before he was safe?

This was a short flight and then we would part ways at a larger airport. I had booked Bez's ticket at the last minute since I wanted to be sure he was going to agree to get on that airplane to our destination. Unfortunately, the flight I had booked for myself by that time was completely full. He and I would have to board at two different gates that would arrive within an hour of each other, with my flight arriving one hour before his. After we had walked into the long hallway where our paths would split, I carefully explained to Bez where his gate was located for boarding and told him I would meet him at his arrival gate at our destination. He nodded without any concern and headed that way after I pointed in the direction he would need to go. I watched him stride confidently down the heavily trafficked corridor and hoped with quiet prayers that he would make it to the next airport alive. I tried not to think about the fear that kept creeping into my heart.

Sure enough, there he was as scheduled when his plane arrived where I was waiting for him! After picking up my suitcase from the belt we walked half a mile to my parked car, climbed in and headed for home. Immediately Bez had other plans. He didn't want me to drive the fastest route, he wanted me to detour along the front range of the mountains. At that point he told me he wanted us to pick up one of his friends along the way to take him back to our town. This friend was one of those I suspected had been using heroin before Bez left the area and I truly did not want him to be around my son. But competing priorities caused me to give in. I needed to get Bez back home with me and, importantly, I had to work the next day. I was already tired before the 4- or 5-hour drive began. Since Bez had agreed to be in detox by the end of the week, I hoped this contact with his old friend from high school would be a positive experience for him in preparation for getting sober. I was dealing with work and home pressures that required attention and I knew that despite my best efforts I couldn't control Bezzy's decisions anyway.

The next day I called my health insurance company again and asked for the names of rehab facilities that were within my insurance company's network. What I discovered is that drug rehab facilities will not accept a patient who has not already detoxed. People who are ready to be admitted into rehabilitation are past the withdrawal stage and are stone cold sober. Unfortunately, this requirement is a major barrier for people caught in the web of opioid use disorder (OUD). So, the next step wasn't rehab, the next step for Bez was detox.

It was a lot of phone calls later that I found a detoxification facility in a suburb of Denver that would probably admit my son in five days' time.

They said that they would expect full payment of five-thousand dollars in cash on arrival.

Just to be clear, I asked again, "Will you accept my health insurance to cover this expense?"

The answer was, "No, we never work with insurance companies; this is cash only."

In addition, I was instructed to call back daily to make sure that he was still on their waiting list. I was incredulous. Is this really the best that medicine can offer a person addicted to heroin? Holy cow.

The rehab center that was in-network for my health insurance plan was recommending this detox facility. But my insurance wouldn't reimburse me for the out-of-pocket expense of detoxing which was a pre-requisite for rehab. When I asked for the rationale, I was told that detox from opioids is not life threatening, so it didn't merit coverage. So, I was thinking to myself, exactly how many people have $5,000 in cash to hand over to a detox facility to provide the support needed for about five days to satisfy the sobriety requirement for rehab? And given the strength of this addiction, how many people who desperately want to be freed from their chains to opioids would be able to make it to sobriety on their own? This reality was hard for me to accept. It defied reason.

I started sweating again. What if Bez would change his mind before we could get him into detox? What would our options be then? I didn't know how long he would be cooperative with this plan, and this was taking too long.

Bez had agreed to meet a co-worker of mine who worked as a nurse in the local ER. He was my resource and guiding my support for my son. This friend of mine from work had experienced his own addiction, and when recovering he had begun to work helping others. He and my son had a private conversation in our basement's family room. My friend later told me he had been tough on Bez and pointed out to him how important it was to be committed to quitting opioids forever before going into detox and rehab. Bez wanted to get sober, but he was struggling. I knew that taking this step was incredibly hard for him.

I had to work the day that the detox facility had an opening, so Lee drove Bez to the facility. It was a long drive, about 5 hours. Lee told me later that Bez had been in tears when they drove away from our town that day. Bez had said he wanted to visit a friend first to say goodbye, but my husband was firm and had said, "No, it is time to go."

Upon their arrival at the detox facility, Lee told me he paid the cash required and left Bez in their hands. To my son's credit, he kept his word and cooperated with the admission process. No communication was allowed between us and our son during his stay there. After four days we heard from his detox facility that he was sober and ready for rehab. Bezzy would be transferred the next day. The in-patient rehab center would pick him up and transport him to their facility in a southern suburb of that city and help start him on the road to recovery.

While he was there, I would get a call from the billing office at the rehab center once a week to inform me of the decision for or against an extension of support from my health insurance company. We didn't know from one week to the next whether he would meet their criteria for additional treatment as an in-patient.

Ultimately, Bez did spend 21 days in this rehab facility where he underwent group sessions and individualized counseling to prepare for sober living. He was originally started on buprenorphine/naloxone when he was in detox but that was discontinued within one week after he entered in-patient rehab. In recent conversations about this time in his recovery, Bez has shared with me the message he internalized which was that the medication he was prescribed was a crutch. He told me he was determined to not fail at sobriety, so he didn't want to use this treatment medication long term. He felt at that time that it was a sign of poor character to require a treatment drug to get off heroin successfully. Bez was determined that he should recover the right way, not the way that weak people would choose. He didn't want to be considered a failure, so he didn't want to continue to use Suboxone after the rehab program was completed. Because this treatment drug is an opioid he had decided he had to stop using it to be considered successful in sobriety.

The last day Bez was in the program, Lee and I were invited to a large gathering of the participants and staff at the in-patient rehabilitation center where our son was asked to make a statement upon graduating. My husband and I were also asked to talk about our feelings related to Bez and his recovery. I cried on stage, Bez cried too, and Lee had to take over when I couldn't speak anymore because of my tears. I suddenly realized that I had hope again, a feeling that I had thought was never going to return. To see Bez looking happy and healthy was such a change in my reality, I was overwhelmed. Bez was alive and he was determined to stay sober. He said so loud and clear.

His next phase of sobriety was planned by the in-patient rehab center, and it was to occur at another facility in the same suburb. Bez required another 4 weeks of counseling and close monitoring before he could start looking for work in that community. When he reached the end of this second formal step-down program, he would begin living in one of their supervised sober households. This phase of treatment also required my cash because the health insurance coverage had already topped out.

When Bez was able to go into sober living and start working at a restaurant, he was involved with this community of households for three months. He worked and paid his rent and bought his own food. He was supporting himself.

Five months after he entered rehab, he needed to have two wisdom teeth pulled, and afterwards the oral surgeon prescribed Percocet for pain. How and why did this happen? I tried to remember when I was that age and had the same procedure done in the 1970's. My remembered experience was that the extraction of the 4 wisdom teeth was painful but not so debilitating that I couldn't work the same night in the hotel restaurant where I was a cook. Yes, my cheeks were swollen, and I couldn't smile or talk without pain but I could work. I might have taken some Tylenol for the pain but at that time I had never heard of these prescription pain medications. Why would an oral surgeon be prescribing Percocet for this out-patient procedure that consisted of extracting two wisdom teeth? And additionally, why would Bez be accepting an opioid medication knowing that this would increase his risk of returning to a life of opioid use? These questions occurred to me later when he was, again, using heroin.

Soon after his wisdom teeth were extracted, he was expelled from his sober living household because, he told me, he didn't mow the lawn on time. That is when I started helping him with his rent because he had to live on his own. Apartments go for a premium in the city. He had arranged to get a two-bedroom apartment with a friend he had met in the sobriety program that followed rehab. His friend was motivated to continue in her recovery, and she worked hard to keep her job. She had children and due to her own history of OUD, she needed to demonstrate to the court that she could care for her children responsibly.

Bez was not working then except for providing childcare for his roommate's preschool daughter. He should have been looking for work himself. Much later Bez told me that he was telling me lies about looking for work and getting interviews. Why didn't he tell me the truth? Recently, he has leveled with me about his taking advantage of my concern for his well-being at that point in his recovery. It was a difficult time of transition, and he was too far from home. It was too easy to mislead me and thus avoid the difficulties of working.

That autumn, Bez had two uncles, one from each side of his family, who died young, both after lengthy difficult illnesses. He traveled back to Indiana for the first funeral by himself on Amtrak and then picked up his trusty Chevy and brought it back to our state. He rode along with me and Lee a month later when we headed east for the second funeral. By then he was back to using heroin, but he wasn't telling me the truth about it. Much later when I inquired why he had started using this drug again after the succeeding with sobriety for a period of months after rehab, he said, "It was my coping mechanism. I hadn't learned any other method yet to deal with the emotional pain of losing my favorite uncles."

Nineteen months earlier, my older brother had been diagnosed with a deadly brain tumor. When he, his wife and children had received this terrible news, he was immediately evaluated by all the necessary specialists to develop the best treatment plan that medicine could offer. Our family had traveled to surround him with love and support. Lee, Bezzy and Frankie had been sitting in the waiting room with me as we all awaited the completion of my brother's first brain surgery, hoping and praying for his full recovery. While we continued to do our best to think positively about the possibility of curing the cancer that my brother was fighting with all his might, Bez had his own silent unacknowledged struggle that was threatening to take him down.

Eventually, my beloved brother lost his life to a glioblastoma that could not be stopped despite all the expertise of neurosurgeons, oncologists, and regular infusions of love from family and friends. By then Bez was back to using heroin but he wasn't telling me the truth when I asked. In my grief over losing my brother, I wasn't looking for more complications in my life and I don't think I was aware of the subtle changes in his appearance and behavior.

The day that we all gathered to say farewell, Bez was with me in the kitchen at Jake and Nancy's house when the evening arrived. My brother's family had many long-time friends who had supported them through his difficult days of treatment for brain cancer and they had come to grieve with us. Throughout the afternoon and into the night hours good food was shared to give us the strength to keep going forward, priceless memories were spoken, and songs were sung honoring a person so precious to all of us. Most of the family and guests had left by the time my tears could no longer be contained. If the lateness of the hour hadn't already chased them off, my uncontrollable sobbing certainly did. I will never forget that there was one strong friend who held my hand tightly while my sweet Bez had my back, standing directly behind my chair. When the pain had begun to subside and my sobbing faded, only then would Bezzy move away into another room. After I was able to pull myself together, my friend Linda Stucky said to me, "He loves you." I knew she was right.

I got a call from Bezzy's apartment roommate a month later saying that she had to leave to get away from Bez and his heroin use. Although this wasn't entirely unexpected because his stories again didn't add up, I was devastated. There just weren't a lot of options to choose from at that point. He had been through detox, in-patient rehab in two different programs, and sobriety-living while working for several months quite successfully. What was missing? Why had he gone back to heroin use?

Although tempted to bring him back to our town again where I would be able to see him more regularly and give him emotional support, I wasn't optimistic that he would be able to stay away from the drug dealers and users he was familiar with in this place where I lived and where it all began. But he couldn't live alone. What could I do to help him?

At that time, I had just been diagnosed with an early-stage breast cancer and was facing an unknown future myself. I scheduled my surgery right before a previously planned vacation which meant that I would have two weeks to recover before I returned to work.

By then Bez had made a new friend who wanted to move in with him in his apartment. His other friend had already left to protect herself from drug users, and I applauded her determination. Bez wanted to stay where he was, and I didn't have a better alternative for him. He said he and his friend would both be able to stay sober and they insisted they would find work to support themselves.

I said, "Okay, let's give that a try," as I was unwilling to upend his current living situation.

I invited Bez to spend some time with us at home over the Christmas holiday season. It seemed like it might give me some time to talk with him to help figure out next steps to get his recovery back on track. As it turned out, it was wonderful to have him visiting us in our home during that difficult time of facing my own mortality. Bezzy and Lee nursed me back to health in such a loving way. I recall my son at my bedside, cheering me as much as he was able, insisting that I keep a positive outlook despite my new diagnosis. I stayed optimistic since the cancer was found early and the prognosis was good. He had so much fun decorating the house for Christmas while I watched from the couch. He also helped his stepdad prepare the festive dinner and then set the table where we joined hearts and were joyful to be together.

Every chance Bez had to make things beautiful in his environment, he would do that. He had a distinctively visual creativity and I have always enjoyed his tutelage in both my clothing selections as well as interior design. I didn't know where he would go with these natural talents, but he most definitely could have a professional engagement in that realm.

Bez went back to Denver after two weeks and resumed his life there. As it turned out, he was sober while staying with us as I had insisted, and he desperately wanted to do the right thing. When he returned to his apartment, he told me later, he confided to his roommate that he was struggling every day with his desire to use heroin. He said the distraction of his addiction is what was preventing him from focusing on what he knew he needed to do, and that was to get a job to support himself.

His friend who also had a history of drug use advised him that methamphetamine was a drug that he could use that would eliminate the craving for heroin. Bez much later told me that he took this advice and it worked. But of course, it didn't help make things better for him in the long run. Yes, it was a safer drug in the short term because he knew his risk of sudden death was lower, but it was just as bad for him when it came to functioning productively. It was also just as bad if not worse in some respects for his long-term health but with meth there was a better chance of survival until he could figure out how to stay sober without the drugs. Sad to say, Bez then became dependent on methamphetamine.

At that time, Suboxone (buprenorphine/naloxone), the legal prescription drug that would allow an opioid user to function normally without the craving and negative behaviors associated with opioid addiction, was not easy to get because physicians were not widely trained to prescribe it. This was a result of the laws regulating this medication that were very restrictive. Physicians and APP's were not allowed to prescribe buprenorphine without the special training that then allowed the medical provider to receive a certificate from the DEA, called the X-waiver. There had been some diversion of Suboxone onto the streets when it was prescribed too liberally and that sometimes gave this treatment medication a dubious reputation. And, like my son, many people receiving treatment in rehab had been taught that it was a bad thing to need Suboxone long-term to avoid opioid use.

It is now my belief that if he had been encouraged to continue to use Suboxone long term when he went into rehab the first time, his recovery would have been quicker, cheaper, and he would have been able to avoid starting methamphetamine to self-treat his addiction to heroin. Think of how many others who used opioids for the first time without understanding what they were dealing with also have fallen victim to a methamphetamine addiction and have spent additional years spiraling downward.

For Bez, one year after he had entered a very expensive program, everything that he had achieved was disappearing. All told, I asked myself, was this treatment really the best that medical science could offer? Completely clear to me by then was that no person recovering from addiction to opioids could realistically succeed alone. What became the central question for me in my work as a physician was, "How can we do this better?"

I had thought that what had been available to him in Denver was going to give him a better chance to work, a better chance to meet people that would connect with him meaningfully, a better chance at maintaining sobriety than what was available in our small town. But finally, there he was, again living the life of an addict, this time unable to quit using methamphetamine.

I had heard and read a lot of stories about the repeated in-patient rehab treatments that people with opioid use disorder had to complete before they were able to quit using these incredibly addictive drugs. And even after recovery, permanent remission was never a guarantee. The patient with the addiction is blamed for the failure. Having watched my son go through rehab, then attempt to reconnect with productive society, the difficulties encountered with recovery are clearer to me now.

The stigma of addiction makes it harder for the person with this disease to maintain the on-going support that is necessary for long-term recovery. Because the person with the disease is blamed for their addiction, the depression that occurs during separation from loved ones results in self-hatred and suicide. Many times, death occurs because of accidental overdose when the disease is not treated with Suboxone long-term. In so many cases, tragically, families are torn apart permanently because of the trauma to relationships. There are many factors that contribute to the complexity of recovery from this disease.

Largely because of what research has shown neuropsychiatrists and psychologists about the pathophysiology of addiction, there has been improvement in the scientific understanding of treating people with this diagnosis during the past twenty years. What research has shown is that drugs like heroin and methamphetamine change the brain after the first exposure (yes, the first exposure!) making it harder than anyone previously suspected to step away from these highly potent drugs voluntarily.

Think about all those prescriptions containing opioids to treat pain that were taken innocently by millions of patients for decades. As research has continued over the past twenty years, medical providers now have a different view, based on the evidence provided. Buprenorphine as a treatment for opioid use disorder, prescribed carefully and without judgment, must continue for as long as it is needed. Many with OUD may need to take this medication daily for the rest of their lives to prevent a recurrence of opioid use.

Chapter 7

2016—DESTROYED BY METHAMPHETAMINE
AND LOSING JODI TO HEROIN

Not long after my return to work following surgery for breast cancer, I went to Denver for a meeting. I stopped in to visit Bez and found him in a terrible condition of which I was not previously aware due to our contact being limited to occasional phone calls. Bezzy was hallucinating and having trouble walking on his own. The friend who had encouraged him to use methamphetamine to get away from heroin was his roommate at that time. I didn't know for sure that they were using meth, but I could read between the lines. I had already seen quite a few cases in the ER in my town, providing me with observed clinical knowledge of the effects of this devastating illegal drug.

Bezzy was in constant motion, and he was frightened. His anxiety was difficult to watch, and I was almost convinced that he was possessed. He and his roommate kept talking about visions of the devil and spirits, which scared me too. I knew better given my own spiritual references but the horror they were experiencing was contagious.

This is the first time I began to wonder if Bez had a serious mental illness, but as a physician I knew that he would not be able to get any mental health assistance without achieving sobriety first. I called a nurse practitioner with whom I worked to ask if she would take him as a patient if I brought him back home with me. When she agreed I then explained to Bez that he would have to come back to live with me in our small town. I just couldn't justify paying for his apartment without his contributing towards his own support. Additionally, I didn't think it was safe or him to be so far from my watchful monitoring. His mental and physical health were not good.

Bez agreed to return with me but he asked if his roommate could come with him since they both wanted to get sober. I realized that if I said no to his friend joining our household and if I stopped paying the rent on their apartment in the city, Bez would probably be gone from us forever. Knowing that this privileged kid of mine was not equipped to survive homelessness, I did not think that tough love and risking his life to make a point was the right plan. I did not want him to become a statistic of the streets and I knew that he could perish because of coldhearted pragmatism. If I turned my head away and let him die while knowing the risk, I don't think I could ever recover emotionally from the unnecessary and preventable death of my own son. It was a deliberate and calculated decision on my part, realizing the risk of judgment from friends and family who were already distancing themselves.

He was mentally ill without question. I did have a choice and I thought that Bez could work with mental health and addictions treatment opportunities in an out-patient setting in our town. Just in case he would consider undergoing more in-patient rehabilitation, I offered this as well, but he refused. He told me he had already learned all that they could teach him. He promised that he would get sober, stay sober, start working and he would support himself. His roommate said he would do the same and they would both support themselves. Lee and I agreed on the condition that Bez would seek mental health treatment and that they would both cooperate with drug testing that Lee and I would request of them randomly. If they resumed using meth or any other illegal recreational drug, they would be looking for a different place to live.

Back to our town they came.

Bez looked better after he was started on anti-depressant medications that had been prescribed by my associate nurse practitioner. His difficulty sleeping was also improving. This was very encouraging because it meant that there was less need for self-medicating with street drugs. If he was still using meth, it was only small amounts, and he was coherent, able to function much better than he had been in the city on his own. He got a job at Walmart and he liked that job. He was assembling bicycles and organizing the children's toy section. However, his friend wasn't gainfully employed, and he would spend his days in the basement of our home alone. Once, I came home from my job and found him going through my husband's old treasures that were stored in a basement closet.

I was surprised by this behavior and couldn't stop myself before I asked incredulously, "What on earth are you doing?"

He said, "I am organizing your things and storing them better."

I was so shocked by his assuming he could take this liberty with our private things that I could not put together a reasonable response. I was dumbfounded. I wanted him out! Even Lee was losing patience by then and he didn't trust either Bez or his roommate. Feeling like Bez was making progress I struggled because I didn't want to force him to leave. Where would he go? I wanted to have more time for Bez to get a handle on this working and living in sobriety challenge that he had taken on. His room-mate was a different question because the weird behaviors and his non-compliance with our original agreement was seriously problematic for us, but this was a young adult who did not have the support of his parents and he had nowhere else to go. Our town did not have sobriety housing to offer anyone who needed that kind of safety from the drugs available in the community. What could we do?

One of the people with whom Bez had reconnected upon returning to Lamar was Jodi, the stunningly beautiful girl that he had known from high school days. She had been one of the friends with whom he had double dated, and he had gone to prom with her. At the time, he had been a new-comer in this school district and their relationship was special.

It was a bit over five years later when I was working in the Emergency Department that Jodi came in as a patient. Still sweet and beautiful, I greeted her and remembered her friendship with Bez. This, however, was not a social call. She told me her difficult story since I had not had a conversation with her for some years. She revealed that she had been struggling with sobriety and explained to me that she was preparing to go into detox for opioid use disorder. The court required her to complete her withdrawal from heroin in a supervised setting and then she needed to finish an in-patient drug rehabilitation program successfully to return to her job which was a requirement for her to resume parental custody of her baby daughter. She needed my help before she entered the court's detox program because she would not have medical providers on site. She asked me for prescriptions so that she could have the medications that might help her tolerate the withdrawal she would experience there.

I wanted so badly to help her succeed. I remember the earnest conversation we had together that day. She was so hopeful that this time she would be able to get off the heroin and stay free of the drug. She told me about her daughter to whom she wanted to return and she was optimistic that she would succeed. There is no question in my mind that if will power alone could make it happen, she would have been able to get heroin out of her life. I prescribed for her what our medical references were recommending for symptomatic treatment of withdrawal from opioids, but I knew these medications would not eliminate the craving and the endless distraction of yearning for the drug that is described by people with this disease. Jodi was thankful for my efforts on her behalf and privately I prayed for her success. At that time no physicians in our group were prescribing Suboxone and our hospital's formulary did not offer access to this medication in the ER. An induction was not an option. As a result, I could not give her the one drug that could have saved her life.

It was about two months later that Bez ran into the house shouting to me that Jodi had died of a heroin overdose. Between his sobs he said she had recently been released from jail and someone had provided her with heroin. I was devastated. Bez was grief stricken. We were both stunned, horrified, and heartbroken. I felt that I was to blame because I had not been able to prevent her death. I was most likely the last physician to care for her before she died of this highly stigmatized, treatable disease.

As a physician I then realized how ineffective my profession was in dealing with the growing opioid epidemic and the ever-increasing deaths. Jodi's death convinced me that we *had* to do better; we *had* to learn how we could treat this difficult disease to get better outcomes. As a physician I owed it to this community to find a better way. This small town was drowning in the deaths of its gorgeous and talented youth and nothing we were doing at that time was making a difference.

Bez was getting counseling as he had promised. His behavioral health therapist was telling him that he needed to get away from our town to be able to stay sober. Lee and I pondered that advice. Where could he go? Should we move to another location as well to support him? Could Bez make it on his own without our moral support, love, and encouragement close at hand?

One condition of his moving back into our home with his roommate was that they had agreed to provide urine for drug tests whenever we asked. That wasn't happening as planned. So, finally, after about nine months of togetherness we told Bez and his roommate that it was time to leave. I suggested they could possibly go to where Bezzy's dad lived. Jobs were booming there, and anyone would be able to find work. They should be able to support themselves in that environment and pay their own way.

The two of them agreed to pack up and leave after Christmas. They kept their word and got on the Amtrak headed for Chicago with their backpacks and extra layers of clothing to survive the winter's cold. A frigid and bone-chilling wind had been blowing as we waited outside the station for the train to arrive. I thought about what lay ahead for them with the wind and temperatures likely to be even worse when they disembarked in Chicago.

At this point, Bez seemed to have a good relationship with his dad and stepmother, and I was counting on that to help stabilize him and his roommate as they began a new chapter in an environment that was familiar to Bezzy. Whether they would find acceptance as they struggled to become a part of that community was not a certainty.

Chapter 8

2017–2018—HENRY TAKES A TURN

WHEN MY YOUNGEST SON and his roommate left our town after Christmas, Bez's dad gave them a place to live in an apartment building he owned. Both started jobs and things were going well at first; Bez was paying Henry rent from his earnings, and that seemed to signal success.

Things started to crumble after some months and from the distance between us I heard about badness happening when Bez's dad began taking sides against him in the rental house disputes. It was a large historic mansion that had been carved up into four apartments. Bez was angry that his dad was not trusting what he was saying, and he felt that Henry was easily manipulated by the other apartment dwellers. It appeared to me from a great distance that the other tenants were trying to push Bez out and they were forcing a wedge between him and his father. It was not a good omen to hear that Bez had lost his dad's favor.

In addition to Bez's sadness about the loss of his relationship with his father, there were some dynamics between Bez and new friends he had made in the community that also had me concerned. In the summer of 2017 when I visited, he and his new friends were moving out of the apartment he had been renting from his dad. He had not brought his worn-out Chevy when he moved back to the Midwest, and he needed transportation for work so I bought him a used sports utility vehicle. This was the one thing I could do for him that could help him continue to work to support himself.

By the end of that year, Bez had been evicted and he had no place to live. Sadly, he had lost his favorite job at a restaurant in an awful situation that involved the police. He was trying to be brave, but I heard desperation in his voice. Honestly, I was beginning to fear for his life.

I am not habituated to dealing with the drug underworld and the lives of those who have spent time in prison. I didn't know how much of what he was doing involved hardened criminals, but I understood that illegal drugs in the mix of any set of activities increases the potential for violence. You will recall that violence is not okay with me at all.

I was, for the first time, worried that Bez was going to wind up dead due to some kind of drug related dispute. I would talk to him regularly on the phone and he would try to reassure me that everything was fine. By this time his dad had completely withdrawn from the parental team. I was hearing from my relatives who encountered Bezzy on the streets of that town, saying that he looked homeless and extremely emaciated. Again, I felt that another change had to happen to prevent an inevitable progression of his downward spiral and the possibility of losing him forever. Since there was no one else in his life willing to give him a chance to start over I knew it would be up to me and I hoped I could persuade my sympathetic but often pessimistic husband to try again to give a hand.

Next time visiting the area where he was living in 2018, I explored with Bez the possibility of coming with me again to Colorado. Really unsure of what to do we talked about it at great length. We both knew that many of his old friends still using drugs in my town would try to pull him back into their lives if he returned. Not having anything better to offer him, and still with no sobriety housing in our region, I eventually invited him and promised I would again try to help him by supporting him emotionally and financially with conditions that Lee and I expected him to meet. He said he would get an apartment on his own this time and would not require me and Lee to open our home. His understanding that he needed to be in his own space seemed to be a more mature attitude than he had had before. That seemed to be a hopeful and encouraging sign.

We said, "Okay let's try again."

Chapter 9

2019–2020—NEVER GIVE UP

IT WAS A FALSE hope that Bez could make a go of sobriety in our town. Like witnessing Jodi's vow to recover, I believe he tried his best but will power alone was not enough. Although methamphetamine did not have a treatment drug like Suboxone for opioid users, the lessons physicians were learning from the neuroscientists demonstrated a similar problem of this addiction compared with that of opioids. Desire to be free of the drugs and the risks that came with them was not enough to prevent him from associating once again with the people who knew his weakness. They couldn't resist pulling him into their world. They knew who his mother was and they needed what his access to money and resources could potentially offer them as well. Unfortunately, on his side of the dependent relationship, he needed their access to a drug. At that point for him it was always methamphetamine.

He and his friend did find their own place to live out in the country but unfortunately, as it turned out, their landlord was also a meth user and the three of them began to have disagreements. This wasn't going well and one night I was summoned by Bez to come over when he became frightened by his landlord's threats. He and his friend had to move out in a hurry and Bez had called the Sheriff's Department for help. The deputy said as I walked into the apartment, "Hey, Dr. Loewen, what are you doing here?"

Bez and his friend ended up back at our house which we had hoped would be a temporary safety measure. His landlord was threatening me as well insisting that Bez owed him money. I knew this was untrue because I had receipts that Bez had gotten from him when they paid the rent. I blocked the landlord's calls and messages and eventually the harassment ended.

About a year after they returned to Lamar, Bez and his friend had to be banned from our home for not keeping their word on drug testing. Lee and I were done. We just couldn't keep living with the lies and the obvious drug use. None of us had any realistic idea of what to do next to help Bez and he was back to living in his vehicle on the streets, this time in our own community. We were sick at heart and wishing for a solution when he was arrested one night. His taillight on one side had some broken plastic covering the light bulb. The police report said the bright white light coming from that taillight was a hazard to other drivers. It had been cracked when Bez backed into something accidentally. I had asked him repeatedly to get it repaired, knowing it was one thing that would eventually get him pulled over by the local police.[1]

Sure enough, that was the pretext under which he got pulled over. In his desperation, just possibly that might have been a subconscious motive for leaving it unrepaired. It is hard for me to know and even Bezzy admits now that it is impossible from this distant vantage point to remember clearly what was in his mind.

Bez had been spotted hanging out with a man who was probably known to the police department as a meth dealer, and he gave this man a ride somewhere that evening. When meth was found in his vehicle, Bez and his passenger were both arrested and they both went to jail. Their booking photos appeared at the top of the front page of our town's newspaper a few days later.

Later that week a local contractor who had agreed to renovate our three bathrooms called to cancel the contract. My husband asked why he had changed his mind, and the contractor offered no explanation. Soon after, I was at the grocery store and crossed paths with the contractor's wife with whom we had spent significant time selecting colors and designs of fixtures that would be installed in our bathrooms. I attempted to greet her. She saw me and immediately averted her eyes. Then, changing her facial expression into a tight-lipped mask she rudely walked by me after quickening her pace without speaking.[2]

Prowers County was not one where drug-related arrests were considered any differently than criminal activities. There was no drug court to

1. Olorunnipa and Witte, *Born with two strikes,* Washington Post.
2. Volkow, *Stigma and Toll of Addiction,* 1289–90.

provide a different kind of solution for these defendants than the punishments that were expected following criminal convictions. After Bez was arrested, I offered a statement at the sentencing, thinking that I would be part of the team that would help plan steps for his recovery from substance use disorder. At the encouragement of his court-appointed attorney, there were letters that had been submitted by Bezzy's friends supporting him, letters written by community leaders who knew him and liked him, there were letters from his friends in other communities vouching for his character where he was also known and loved. What I didn't expect was that as his mother I would be vilified by the judge as the cause for his drug addiction. What happened in court stunned me.

The judge said in his summary to Bez while I listened in remotely during the court's conference call, "So you were probably . . . you were dealt somewhat of a bad hand. A mother who gave you up for adoption. But you had parents who tried to take care of you I believe. And I'm not demeaning your mother or your stepfather or your father, but they love you so much that I think they've enabled you to be what you're like right now . . . I think you're probably a really nice kid, but something gone (sic) haywire here."[3]

Weirdly and coincidentally, I had heard Dr. Jerome Adams, then Surgeon General of the United States, say at the Colorado Hospital Association's Opioid Summit in Denver six weeks earlier ". . . that the shame heaped on the heads of parents of children with addiction is what contributes to the stigma that surrounds them and prevents their child's recovery."

At that conference in February of 2020, Dr. Adams told the story of his own brother imprisoned, serving a 10-year sentence for stealing two-hundred dollars to support his opioid addiction. Dr. Adams said that generally the family is blamed for creating the addicted child. The spoken and unspoken assumption is that there was something that happened in the home, usually a lack of discipline, that is attributed as the source of the addiction.

Dr. Adams had said, "You know most people would think that a family that had produced a Surgeon General was a pretty good family. Think about this: my parents produced a child who became a Surgeon General and a child who became an opioid addict. Does that mean my parents are to blame for the disease of addiction that my brother is struggling with?"

The next speaker on the program at this conference continued to say, "As a white man, if I had been arrested for stealing two-hundred dollars,

3. Court documents, public domain.

I would have gotten a slap on the hand and a stiff lecture from the judge with a requirement to pay back the victim and then I would have been released. Look at the inequity that exists in the courts of this country! A young black man is serving ten years in prison, the brother of the Surgeon General of the United States, the harshest of punishments that is provided for the worst criminals, for being a victim of the disease of addiction."

Was it true? Was the judge at Bez's sentencing correct to think that my son's addiction was my fault? Did Bez's recent diagnosis of bipolar disorder, only partially treated at the time of his arrest, carry any weight in the judge's consideration? Did Bez's biracial physical appearance contribute to his sentence, harsher than a lighter skinned, straight-haired man would have received? In the first place, would a white man in our town have been pulled over for having a broken taillight that would ultimately lead to his being arrested and sentenced to 42 months of incarceration in a community corrections facility with his judge complaining that he couldn't send him to the penitentiary because it was his first offense? All these questions were difficult for me to reconcile given the reality that I have experienced as a person with privileges that all people should be accorded equally. To paraphrase the judge, something definitely " . . . gone (sic) haywire here."

As I wrote this segment of our story, I was packing Bez's bags for his transfer from the county jail to the community corrections facility in a distant town. With good behavior and evidence of an ability to function drug-free, he could have an opportunity for the minimum period of incarceration which was likely to be two more years in addition to the six months already served in jail, according to the prediction of his attorney. I was mending his favorite plaid pajamas from his Aunt Nancy, given to him during our family Christmas gift exchange some years previously. I sewed as much love into every stitch as I could while patching his pajamas that day, praying for his success as he entered the next important stage of his young life.

The fury and anguish I experienced after the court proceedings of the day before caused me to turn a corner. It brought a conscious realization that my time in this remote community was approaching an end. My job here was nearly done. I understood then that I was not accepted in this town at least in part for being the mother of a young man who was struggling to live in recovery, and even more than that, being punished subtly by some for helping him. There were too many negative vibes. I thought I might be tolerated if I stayed under the radar. If, on the other hand, I made waves and rocked that prairie schooner culture hard enough to break one of its archaic wooden wheels, I would perhaps present enough of a threat to merit old fashioned methods to remove an undesirable element. This was a traditional town of the Far West. That episode with the judge was, for me, the last straw and I felt exposed, vulnerable, and alienated from the community that I had tried so hard to help, that I had tried so hard to make my forever home.

As that day became many days of waiting for Bez to be released from the county jail and reading more about stigma in research studies that addressed this phenomenon, I learned that it prevents people from standing with their brothers, sisters, sons, daughters, cousins, grandsons, granddaughters, dads, moms and neighbors in an expression of love and support, which is a critical component of recovery.[4] It was now post-sentencing day eleven and Bez was not yet transferred out of jail to the community corrections facility.

On top of everything else happening to my son, Covid-19 had gotten in the way of life-as-usual for the incarcerated. I spoke with an administrative staff member at his soon-to-be community corrections center after Bez's sentencing and was told that the authorities would not allow any admissions there until the social distancing requirements had been lifted. My son told me on the phone that the usual fifty to sixty inmates at the jail had been thinned down to about thirty, and he was one of them.

Fortunately, Bez had a job in the jail. After six weeks of exemplary behavior as a kitchen worker, he had been elevated to the coveted position of the head trustee. He had worked previously as a cook in several restaurants, and he told me he really enjoyed this part of his day. He was blessed to have this outlet for his energy and creativity. From my perspective, imagining the daily routine of jailhouse life, he was doubtless a help and a source of cheer to those around him. One of the guards with whom I was acquainted through Bezzy's introduction told me that he was brushing up on his Spanish while working with the cooks, and all were loving that interaction.

The wait for him to be released to community corrections took months. What was so hard on me was not having any opportunity to visit with him in person. Our visits were limited to the phone service that was offered for a considerable price by the jail. Or, if I would stand in line in the visitors' lobby, I could get connected on a public video phone that made it possible to see his face while we spoke. That was the closest I could get to

4. McGinty and Barry, *Stigma Reduction*, 1291–92.

being with him during that long period of months. I missed my Bez just terribly, whom I loved so dearly.

My challenge during this time was to stay calm, to accept my task, and to be a blessing in my work environment as well. I was the Medical Director for Prowers Medical Center's Emergency Department which involved organizing the care our team of emergency physicians was providing for this region. Before Covid arrived, I had been learning about Suboxone, the opioid-containing medication, also known as buprenorphine/naloxone generically, used exclusively to treat opioid use disorder.

I had taken the necessary full day of training to be authorized to prescribe this medication, which at that time required the certificate called an X-Waiver from the DEA. At that training session I had learned about many emergency departments across the country that were offering help for people with opioid use disorder when they were in withdrawal and desperately trying to stay sober. The more I learned the more interested I became in developing a protocol for our ER to offer this treatment for our patients who were addicted to opioids. This disease was killing more people every year and now, as emergency physicians, we could access the medication that would prevent deaths by starting the treatment they needed when they were ready for sobriety.

The next step was to develop a partnership in our town with an outpatient addictions clinic so that after being started on Suboxone in our ER, those persons would be referred to specialists for long-term care appropriate for their individualized needs. We didn't have an out-patient clinic in our town willing to prescribe Suboxone so networking to develop that capacity was the first step. In addition, offering the new treatment for opioid use disorder required our hospital's administrative team to be educated on the facts of this disease, the rising disaster of mental and physical dysfunction, drug related crimes, and deaths from overdoses in our community. However, before I could approach our hospital's Board of Directors to request the addition of this treatment to our scope of care, I needed to have the clinical out-patient care network in place.

While continuing the behind-the-scenes work on developing this state-of-the-art treatment for opioid use disorder, I continued to help our hospital prepare for what was coming with Covid-19. There was so much that we didn't yet know about the new respiratory disease that was producing severe systemic consequences. If our region was unable to flatten the rising curve of infections, we expected that the larger medical centers in the big cities on the front range of the Rocky Mountains might be filled to capacity. People from our corner of the state would not have any place to go for the advanced care they would need to survive.

Our best defense from this communicable disease was prevention of the spread through airborne viruses, but this was a concept that often fell on deaf ears in this community. Most felt that wearing a mask somehow infringed on their freedoms. Some of the patients that knew and trusted me as a physician listened to my urgent message of the need to prevent Covid's highly contagious spread, but more in our town were defiant, often with deaths occurring among their church friends, workplaces, and extended families as a result. It was tragic to watch because these illnesses and deaths were in large part preventable and as a physician, I felt so ineffective due to having so little influence.

One night I arrived in the ER to begin my night shift and was informed by the outgoing physician that there was a dead person in our trauma bay awaiting the coroner's visit before being taken to a funeral home. I put on my head-to-toe protective garments to say hello to the family that was assembled at that deceased person's bedside. The trauma bay was full of relatives, none of whom were wearing masks. I left the room after taking a brief look and headed back into the area where patients came out of triage and picked up a handful of masks to distribute among the family members. Before heading back into the trauma bay I talked to the clerk at the front desk and asked why all those people had been allowed to enter without masking? No answer was offered. Since the requirement to cover one's nose and mouth upon entry to the hospital was plastered on every wall, I was surprised by the matter-of-fact disregard for the safety rules by the visitors and even the ER staff members on that particular night. The fact that the cause of death for the individual awaiting transport to the funeral home was unknown, also was a source of concern; our hospital's protocol to pre-vent bringing Covid-19 into our safe work setting was being ignored. If the deceased person had died of Covid, how many of the people at the bedside had already been exposed themselves? How many were actively spreading the Covid virus into the air we would all be breathing that night in the ER?

Heading back to speak to the family of the deceased with my handful of masks, I saw the coroner entering the ER correctly wearing a mask per protocol. He was accompanied by a Sheriff's deputy who was not masked. I followed the two men back into the trauma bay and distributed masks to the family as well as the Sheriff's deputy and then left the room.

A few minutes later I walked by that room and peaked in to see how everyone was doing, wondering what the plan was for transport of the corpse out of the ER. At that point I realized that the Sheriff's deputy had not put on the mask I had handed him but had hung it defiantly on one ear. I approached him and waited politely until I had his attention and then quietly informed him that he needed to wear the mask properly over his nose and mouth or he would have to leave the ER.

This massively muscular male, more than six feet tall, two-hundred and fifty-plus pounds and with a service gun in his belt towered over me and said with emphasis, "I have business to take care of and I am not leaving the ER."

I calmly informed him, "You can go outside with the people that you need to talk to."

I was ignored.

The coroner standing next to him with his mask in place leaned towards me and said, "And how about your nurse?"

I turned around and behind me I saw that the registered nurse on duty that night had removed his mask as well as if in solidarity with the deputy. The security guard who had been near the entrance to the ER when I arrived was now absent. It was me alone, at roughly half the body weight of the Sheriff's deputy, about a foot shorter in height and without a firearm in my waistband, laying down the law in the ER where I was responsible for the safety of the patients and the staff that worked there. That was the night the radiology tech who was an ultrasound specialist sat with me in the physicians' workroom and told me how sorry she was about the whole scenario she had witnessed from a distance.

That was also the night that I wrote my letter of resignation, giving the required 30 days' notice to my employer. I knew it was time to go. I slid the letter under the door of the office belonging to the CEO of the hospital before leaving early the next morning, knowing that she would see it there upon returning to work after the weekend. I had to draw a line in the sand after that fateful night or I knew I would forever regret not taking a stand. There was too much at stake for the hospital and the community.

My boss, Karen Bryant, CEO of Prowers Medical Center eventually persuaded me to stay long enough to complete my contract, so I decided against leaving for more than a year after that confrontation. What made the difference is that she was able to persuade our county's Sheriff to require his deputies to follow the hospital's masking rules. That was enough progress in the right direction to make me feel like our safety rules were going to be respected. After that, the Sheriff's deputies came into the ER with their masks in place, at least when I was on duty.

At that time an additional stressor was that I didn't know how I was going to work in the Covid Intensive Care Unit that our hospital was trying to develop, while I was also scheduled to work in the ER clinically and managing the Emergency Department at the same time. Our shortage of physicians was an unresolvable part of the puzzle. My imagination went wild and there were plenty of times in the isolation of those days of Covid-19 that a better future seemed out of reach.

An unexpected source of encouragement occurred during one of those difficult days when I received an email that was initiated by one of my long-time friends Michele Kellner who had connected each of the women in her circle of friends with a different person in that circle. Each was assigned to provide some transforming light in the form of inspiring words for their assigned recipient. The gift sent to me was a podcast of an interview with the late Mary Oliver whose poem *Wild Geese* was one of those featured in this recorded conversation. This fascinating interview led to my searching for the original verse. So much wisdom in those few words led me to better understand my role in the world, letting me accept my own reality. I felt empowered to complete the tasks for which I was trained and capable of carrying out. Both the thoughtfulness of the gift in addition to the perspective that the podcast provided, helped to steady me as I reengaged with my life.

One of the supports that kept Bez centered on his goal to stay sober in his quest for a new life, were his weekly conversations with a life coach who had been recommended for him by another close friend of mine, Juliet Wiebe. Although Joel Elston lived across the country in Richmond, Virginia, he was willing to guide my son with telephone therapy sessions as Bez waited for the time to pass in jail. This helped him a great deal during his difficult time of waiting because Joel had worked with many others in similar situations. Bez's life coach understood that the time Bez spent in jail could be productive if he had the right messages to help guide his thinking as he prepared for a life outside.

Bez also had the advantage of being treated while in jail by a medical provider who had continued his medications for bipolar disorder, and she was gradually adjusting them to better accommodate his needs. He was very fortunate for her help at this critical time of transition.

One day when I wasn't on duty, Bez was transported from the jail to be evaluated in the ER where I worked. I got a call from the unit clerk letting me know that Bez was there, waiting to be seen. She was one of Bezzy's school friends from his early days in high school in this community. She had gotten permission from the deputy to let me know I could come to the ER to be with him while he was being treated for an injury. When I arrived, he was in a black and white striped short-sleeved jumpsuit, in ankle shackles sitting on a gurney in an examination room. When I reached him there, Bez told me he had just been reading on his bunk bed in his cell at the jail, the top bunk, when he was assaulted by another inmate for no reason. The attacker had grabbed his forearm and was trying to smash it hard enough against the bed railing to break a bone or two. Fortunately, Bezzy had only reacted defensively and was strong enough to prevent any significant injury. The other good news was that his efforts to protect himself didn't get him into any trouble with the jail staff because his reaction to the aggression was self-defense only.

After the ER doc on-duty shared with us the results of his normal X-rays, the nurse bandaged his abrasion but otherwise he was okay. It felt odd to watch him shuffle slowly out of the ER with his shackles dragging and clanking, while he held his cuffed hands together in front. With dignity he smiled, nodded, and said "hello" to everyone watching him from behind the nurses' station as he progressed towards the exit. He was known to all of them as my son. They, in turn, were also kind to him, which of course I appreciated. I thanked the Sheriff's deputy for allowing the unit clerk to give me a call since it was the first time I had seen him in person since he had been incarcerated months earlier.

April 30, 2020 was a day of great blessing. As anyone who has supported a person in recovery knows, the unpredictable ups and downs are what makes life so taxing over a long period of time. This day was five weeks after Bez's sentencing. I don't know why so many asks were answered and in a way that helped progress the goals I had been praying about daily but it caused a perceptible and thankful pause in our lives.

First, Bez had been trying to figure out where his Covid stimulus check was deposited after we had opened his letter one week earlier stating that twelve-hundred dollars had been deposited into his bank account. He was puzzled because his bank accounts had been closed already for months. On this day his check arrived in the mail. He was flat broke, and my husband and I were stretched emotionally and financially. Having this check in hand was a huge boost for all of us. Bez was happy to hand it over to us in partial repayment for his bail costs when arrested.

Second, Bez was transferred to his community corrections treatment center that day and he called me after he arrived at this distant community at exactly 2:00 p.m. when I was literally, phone in hand, preparing to call that facility again to ask what their Board of Directors had decided about Bez's transfer. Incredible thankfulness, tears, and an offering of gratitude in prayer was my response. Bez was healthy and out of the county jail.

Third, I had scheduled a meeting with my hospital's senior leadership team to request permission to develop a program to start Medication Assisted Treatment (MAT) services in the ER. I said, "These people with opioid use disorder are just like us. They are people living in our community and our hospital has pledged to care for all members of this community. Stigma can no longer stand between them and the medication they need to begin their recovery."

Under the leadership of Karen Bryant these administrators became interested in this project. They began supporting my efforts to find a referral organization that would provide out-patient clinic services for our patients who needed buprenorphine prescriptions long term. Stigma had thrown molasses into the gears, in a manner of speaking. The engine that needed to engage to produce change in this community was moving slowly. But finally, we had some traction and hope was coming from our hospital's leadership.

Fourth, Bez's truck was parked in front of our house and already had been advertised with a For Sale sign on it for a couple of weeks. At dusk on this extraordinary day, a young couple stopped to look at it. They knew my husband Lee, connected with him and expressed an interest in buying the truck. This was Bez's promise when we bailed him out of jail the second time after his original arrest. He said he wouldn't ask us to bail him out three times. If he couldn't stay sober after that he would sell his truck, his only asset, so that he could pay us back. Having received one interested party's inquiries, there was hope here as well. His responsible desire to pay for his mistakes was a welcome sign of his recovery in progress.

Fifth, my husband got his first social security check ever, a direct deposit into our bank account. This was a major milestone. It wasn't a large sum, but it would help us keep up with the regular bills of daily life. We felt like he had won the lottery! His life's work as a carpenter and construction site superintendent was being rewarded. Thank you, Uncle Sam, for helping those of us who are aging and becoming less able to work. This makes our future easier to contemplate as we must accept that our engagement with the working world is coming to an end.

The day after this wonderful day of blessings, Bez called me to tell me that I could drop off his clothing at his new community corrections facility in Alamosa and a brief visit would be allowed. My trip to his new location occurred four days after he had arrived there.

I packed his things into the car and headed west, toward the mountains. He had so much clothing! It was hard for me to know what he would need, and I thought that he could sort through it all when I got there. His facility was located more than three hours by car from our town. As I drove, I could not help but remember how far we had come as a family, and I was overcome with thankful emotion. On this day I also recognized that I was receiving a special gift of promise that included a future with my younger son.

Tears had been flowing during these days of inexplicable joy as well as sorrow for a period of months. But this day as I reflected on the future, driving over the crest of one of the foothills, there was a sudden panoramic mountain view so grand that I found with astonishment it was almost too much to take in. It was a solitary experience with no other vehicles on the road as I drove closer to this astonishingly beautiful terrain. I could hardly breathe. Again, my eyes filled with tears, this time with appreciation for the positive forces surrounding me and Lee as well as Bez, and for keeping us safe in this time of the Covid-19 pandemic.

Bez had been saying, "It is the *power of yes* that will make the difference." He had developed a new attitude about his recovery with the help of his life coach Joel.

After arriving at his new community corrections facility, I saw Bez briefly in the front office. The staff went through all his clothing and other basic items, and he appeared healthy and cheerful. They sent back two of the three suitcases of clothing, allowing Bezzy some input on what stayed with him. Driving back home following this brief supervised visit, Frankie called to ask how his brother was doing. I shared with him the good news about Bez's healthy appearance and optimistic attitude. It was a promising new beginning.

When I arrived back home, under a clear star-filled sky, the evening was cool, and the wind was quiet. Our two dogs, Oliver and Theo, were excited to see me and happy to settle down on our laps as Lee and I talked over the day's events in the warmth of the flames from the fire pit table on the patio. I knew that I would miss these evenings when we had gone from this place.

Bez's first task at community corrections was to get a job. He needed to support himself with his earnings while under staff supervision. He had to pay for room and board as well as the fees for regular drug testing and counseling sessions. Over time he also had to pay for the court costs that resulted from his original arrest.

After three weeks of searching, he was still unemployed. It was heartbreaking for me when he explained that as he filled out job applications, he had to report the felony on his record. He had such a desire to work for Safeway and the store manager had relayed that he wanted to hire him for their available position. He was excited because he thought he would enjoy this work opportunity. In addition, this was a large corporation that promoted from within. He thought there could be a future for him there. Unfortunately, when the regional office saw his felony conviction it was a no go. Bezzy was devastated.

One day after he had almost given up on the job search, an inmate in his corrections facility told Bezzy that the furniture store where he worked was hiring. Bez went to apply for this job, and he was immediately hired. He started work the same day! Bez said he was surprised because he had told the owners his entire story of addiction, arrest and time in jail including the felony on his record. He expected to be turned away but this time the owners of the store said, "You are hired. You can start working right now."

This was the beginning of Bezzy's best job ever. The owners of this furniture store, John and Rhonda Vest, told me when I met them a few weeks later that they saw there was a need in their community. They wanted to help people who deserved a new start. In the case of my son, it was just the boost that he needed. They loved him. He loved them back and learned so much about being a good employee, how to be a successful salesman and how to be accurate at the cash register. He also became their warranty service specialist, so he had to develop skills involving treating customers with kindness and fairness. His life was changing, and he was sober.

I watched Bez as he grew in confidence with his new life in recovery. He now lived in a different town that prioritized their human capital and he was blossoming with the support he received from his job, new friends and counseling that was a requirement of his correctional program. He had hope and he had started thinking about his future.

His self-image was changing as well. One snowy day as spring approached in this mountain community, he walked into town to look for a barber. A police car stopped next to him, and the officer asked if he needed a ride. Bezzy told him he needed a haircut and, yes, he would be happy to accept a ride. The officer drove to his own barber shop and introduced Bez to that establishment. After his arrival on the premises with his new friend Ivan Garcia, Assistant Chief of Police, the barber immediately put Bezzy in the chair and got to work cutting the long curly locks. Bez told me how surprised he was to have this attention and help from a law enforcement officer. This was the beginning of a significant friendship.

Unknown to Bez at the time, the Police Department in this town had developed a partnership with Law Enforcement Assisted Diversion (LEAD), a nation-wide charitable organization that provides a community-based approach for people with drug addictions. The goals of this organization are to improve public safety, public order and to reduce the unnecessary involvement of the justice system among those who qualify for the program. This kind and caring police officer soon recommended Bez to this program thus providing him with on-going support as he progressed through the remainder of his community corrections sentence.

Chapter 10

2021—THE BENEFITS OF SOBRIETY

As a result of Bezzy's good behavior, his release into non-residential status occurred after just nine months in community corrections. This meant Bez did not have to live in the facility any longer, but he still had to call in daily and he needed to report back when instructed for random drug testing. He also had to continue attending individual and group counseling sessions one day a week, on his day off work. This new freedom was wonderful but presented a new problem for him because he didn't have a place to live. For the first month he lived with a friend he had made in this town but after a month Bezzy felt he needed to find new digs because the apartment was too small for two adults, and he didn't want to ruin a friendship by taking advantage.

He had been looking for an apartment, but he couldn't afford the rent anywhere in Alamosa. The community corrections facility still required him to pay for their services and his debt to the courts so there just wasn't enough money left after these were satisfied to be able to move out on his own.

At that point another person he had gotten to know offered Bez a room in his house that he felt he could use only temporarily. This time a larger space was available than where he had been staying, but Bezzy knew it was not a long-term arrangement. This new friend would not accept any payment while he stayed there. Bez was so appreciative of the help he was getting but he knew he had to find a place of his own. He had already grown fond of this town with its welcoming culture and wanted to make this his permanent home.

I traveled to his town in the mountains to visit the weekend before Mother's Day. Bez and I had been combing the ads for apartments on-line for weeks. Again, we looked at the ads together. I knew he could not afford any of the places that were allowing pets. He had his heart set on getting his dog back. Any apartment not allowing pets would not be a workable option. This sweet little dog that my husband and I had kept for Bez all these years with the expectation that someday Oliver would be able to live with his owner again, had to happen soon. This would be one of the most important rewards for my son now successfully living in recovery.

Bez and I sat in my car in the parking lot at Walmart that Saturday, going through all the options available to him. The housing market in the city was so expensive that people who were able to work remotely were moving to rural communities because of the cost of housing in the dense population centers. As the Covid pandemic continued, more and more employees were allowed to work at home which made the cost of living in these lovely mountain locations even more unaffordable for people earning minimum wage. Bez just wanted a safe place to live with his dog. How could I help provide the stability that he needed to be able to succeed as he continued to stay on the path of sobriety? What could I do to make his future more secure as he completed his correctional sentence with plans of staying in this community permanently?

Without any prompting from Bez, an epiphany suddenly arrived. Knowing that I was going to be moving back to the Midwest by the end of the year I would be able to invest the funds from the sale of our property in the other rural community to buy a home for our son in this new location. He would be able to occupy this house with little Oliver while paying us what he could afford to support this expense. Next step would be finding a property that would check all the boxes for me as investor and for Bez as occupant. I needed to think about this overnight before I made any proposal to him.

The next morning waking up in my hotel room, I pushed the drapes aside and looked out at the mountain peaks, realizing I could own a house with this view. It felt like the right decision for so many reasons. I called Lee and explained what had begun to crystalize in my mind with both investment and a housing solution for Bez as motivators. He thought about it, encouraged me to talk to my brother James who might be more objective, asked a lot of questions, and then after multiple conversations agreed with my plan.

I had invited Bezzy for breakfast at my hotel that Sunday morning which was a decent hot meal served by staff from behind the counter. We were all wearing masks and to meet Covid safety rules, we were required to go to my room to take off our masks to eat. We walked past, and remarked about the closed indoor pool, still restricted from access due to the continuing Covid pandemic.

Back in my room, I shared my idea with Bez. He and I sat together imagining this potential future solution for his housing need. We discussed the specifics of what would be possible from my end and from his. We felt we could make this work if we could find the right house. We got to work immediately reviewing the real estate listings on-line. There was not much in my price range. We did find one small house that was a little higher in price than what I had hoped but it was the right size with a fenced-in backyard, and we decided we should drive by this property to look together. After viewing the exterior of the house and the neighborhood where the house was for sale, we agreed it had potential.

I had to stay until Monday to be able to look at this property and fortunately it was possible for me to delay my departure that extra day. The realtor we selected was the one who answered our telephone inquiry that weekend. She said she would try to get us an appointment to view the property quickly. She was able to arrange this and the next day Bezzy came with me while I inspected this house inside and out. He had asked his furniture store bosses if he could arrive at work a little late that Monday so he could accompany me, and they were able to accommodate his request. As it turned out we loved this house which had been recently renovated in a traditional southwestern style. I made an offer that was accepted and then the purchase processes began.

What Bez and I didn't know yet is that this historic property built in the 1920's had become a meth house that had exploded and burned a few years earlier when its occupants were cooking that destructive drug in the kitchen. After this sad event the house was uninhabitable, so it remained vacant, unwanted and a community eyesore for a couple of years. Eventually a couple bought the property for a reported $2,800 and started working on it. They moved in when it was safe to inhabit and continued to make improvements, dedicated to returning this house to its former utility as an attractive and comfortable home. They gradually invested money in the property and rebuilt it as they were able to afford the costs. They wanted it to become completely functional and they kept working on that house for several years before they were ready to sell. By the time they put it on the market and we had our tour, it had more character than a new house and it was a beauty, now a house with so much warmth to offer its inhabitants.

When Bez told me the story that his friends had shared with him about this house he said to me, "This house reminds me of my life. It was destroyed by methamphetamine, and it sat there unappreciated until someone saw beauty in it and thought it was worth saving. The love and attention it received is what made the restoration a success."

As I continued to work in my rural community before my contract with the hospital concluded, I had time to reflect on the future of the region where we had been living. I realized that over a period of eleven years I had learned a lot about the culture and the people. What I observed was that, in general, the generations coming up behind me were faring less well than my generation. Why was that? What I pondered during the long winter months of the Covid-19 pandemic was the fragility of the rural communities surrounding us. What would the future bring for this town and others like it? Why had the financial health and well-being of this community been undermined? What was once a robust if small commercial district now had become a Main Street struggling to survive. Its decline predated the arrival of Covid-19.

The role of opioid addiction and its effect on those who were not supported with treatment to regain their ability to function at work and at home had certainly been problematic and contributed to its on-going demise. This was a worrisome phenomenon that would require every community in a similar economic situation to focus on to prevent further losses. But the problem was bigger with the prevalence of three diagnoses described as the deaths of despair: opioid overdose, suicide, and deaths from alcoholism.

Economists Case and Deaton provide a strong case in their book, *Deaths of Despair and the Future of Capitalism*.[1] What was useful in their analysis from my perspective was the description of the origin of these tragedies. The result of their research is compelling because it matches the reality of what I had witnessed in one of the regions of rural America. They wrote that the social problems faced by small towns with predominantly working-class populations was related to earnings that had stagnated long enough that there had been a loss of hope among many for a better future for themselves and their children.

1. Case and Deaton, *Deaths of Despair*, 154–55.

What they described that has not been fair is that better educated Americans with bachelor's degrees have made steady gains in their earnings over the decades since 1980. Those without bachelor's degrees in general have not had equivalent wage increases during that same period.

According to their research, significant numbers of not only men of color which was expected, but also white men between the ages of 45 and 55 years which was not expected, have died prematurely during what should have been the most productive years of their lives. In my own experience observing the rural community where I lived and worked, I would expand the group at risk to include both genders with many suicides attempted and many succeeding among teenagers and young adults in their twenties and thirties. These individuals for whom I had provided care, struggled mightily, and couldn't find their way forward. Given limited choices, they, like their parents, found that they were not able to anticipate succeeding in the workplace. None of the limited options available to them had provided them with hope for a better future.

There had been this tragedy unfolding in the region and in others like it all over the country for several decades. The observations and recommendations made could provide a blueprint to build a better future for the less educated who live in every state of the union, in cities and rural communities. Case and Deaton recommended that economic change could be brought by those currently benefiting from the status quo. Those of us familiar with these communities who can advocate for change on their behalf should bring these concepts for consideration to policy makers and politicians. Building a case on behalf of those who deserve better than they have gotten is what could generate the changes necessary to bring hope again.

Recent research confirms the problems that are endemic in our small and large communities. Too many preventable deaths are seen in the younger segments of our population. More than twice as many children have died from poisoning including drug overdoses, as from Covid-19 per David Wallace-Wells in an essay published by *The Journal of the American Medical Association* in March 2023. Also, more than three times as many died from suicide, more than four times as many died from homicide, more than five times as many died in car crashes and other transportation accidents.[2]

Survival of remote towns is beneficial to this country with many reasons why the entire country needs these communities to stay well and

2. Wallace-Wells, *It's Deaths of Children*, JAMA Essay.

prosper. As a physician living in one of our country's rural communities for more than a decade, I have so many friends now who grew up in the cultures of El Norte and The Far West regions. These cultures were aptly described by Colin Woodard, whose excellent historical account, *American Nations—A History of the Eleven Rival Regional Cultures of North America*, deserves recognition.[3]

It is unacceptable that so many in this population are suffering and without hope in a country that can afford to make the changes needed to provide a future for all its people. There are economic and educational inequities that have been unavailable for many from these rural communities that require careful consideration and action by our democratically elected politicians.

People with addictions and mental health diseases must be assured that they are needed, to know that there is a role for them in our communities just like there is for every other person. Necessary to their recovery is knowing that they are allowed to make mistakes and that those errors will be forgiven. Stigmatizing people with opioid use disorder and related substance abuse disorders must be overcome. In addition, stigmatizing families who are helping their addicted loved ones should become unacceptable at every level in all communities.

My own childhood was from a different location. As I mentioned earlier, I lived in Congo during the years before and after its independence from Belgium in 1960. The American military had a presence there for several years during the Cold War between 1961 and 1967. Our family lived in the capital city early on, called Leopoldville and later Kinshasa, during most of those years. On Saturday nights we were often invited, as were all the American and Canadian families, to the small military base at the international airport named N'djili just outside Leopoldville to watch movies. We would assemble on the blankets our parents brought as we congregated on the concrete floor of the airplane hangar where the GI's would show Western movies as a treat for the expatriate community. The soldiers were good hosts and they cheerfully served us popcorn and Coca Cola, making it a truly memorable American experience.

Like so many children of that era, we became enthralled with the culture of the Cowboys and Indians displayed on the big screen with the beautiful scenery of the High Plains east of the Rocky Mountains. These movies also displayed the most gorgeous horses and gritty pioneers traveling in

---

3. Woodard, *American Nations— Eleven Cultures*, 23–33 and 243–53.

covered wagon trains in stark contrast with the traditional way of life of the indigenous American Indian tribes. As an adult, I understand now that so much that was stereotypically described in those movies was unfair and insensitive. Having had a chance to learn more about this region by living where these events occurred more than a century ago has been a treasured experience. I have met so many lovely people and I was honored to have been their physician for many years. It has been a good run.

Because of the kindness and love of so many, my youngest son has settled into his new community as a productive member of society. There are many others with opioid use disorder who also deserve a chance to build a future for themselves with our help. I was happy that I could anchor myself and my son with a house that would welcome me back again and again during my visits with him as the future unfolds for us.

Chapter 11

2022—REACHING FOR THE STARS

It was important for Bez to continue to stay motivated to complete his community corrections program with an excellent record. He did succeed in achieving that goal in November of 2022. The court was satisfied that he had repaid his debt to society, and he was released from the correctional system.

Three months before completing that program, he was invited by Carey Deacon, Program Director of Law Enforcement Assisted Diversion (LEAD) in Alamosa to consider a job they were expecting to open for a Case Manager with Lived Experience. This would mean leaving the wonderful furniture store where he had been working for more than two years. This did not mean that he would be any less important to the couple who owned Big John's Furniture Warehouse and who took their role as mentors seriously. John and Rhonda discussed this potential move with him understanding that a professional job with a good salary and benefits could provide the experience that would get him to the next level in his career. They encouraged him to think about this job possibility very carefully. It would mean he would receive an opportunity to have his future higher education paid for as part of the benefits package. There was a known history of employees of this organization going to college part-time, completing their undergraduate degrees over a period of years. As an employee of this organization, he would also be provided time to attend classes as well as time to study, while expenses were covered by this new employer. Bezzy was encouraged by his mentors to apply.

Meanwhile, during the warmth of the seasons before changing jobs there was time for him to drive into the Rocky Mountains that ringed his community to experience the remote high valleys with his mentors on weekends. They treated him like family. Even I was invited to join them where together we enjoyed the peaceful sights, sounds and smells of nature while relaxing on the porch of their cabin next to a remote lake one weekend. Bez and I loved the thrill of the ride provided in an all-terrain vehicle on steep trails to the top of a rounded peak, then rewarded with breathtaking views of the distant mountains. Returning to the valley we followed the trail next to an ice-cold stream that sparkled in the sun. We admired the beauty of a small herd of elk peeking at us with curiosity, groves of pine trees and aspens, quiet ponds hosting all sorts of wildlife and we marveled at snowbanks still slowly melting in the warmth of the summer season. We ate a hearty meal that night and enjoyed lively conversation and entertaining stories with the wood burning stove heating the great room before I headed to the guest quarters to sleep. Bezzy took the couch outside my door and the next morning he said he heard me singing as he fell asleep. We touched the stars that night high in the remotest regions of the Rocky Mountains, cozy in a cabin with dear friends and a fire keeping us warm.

Bez applied for the job with the Law Enforcement Assisted Diversion program in Alamosa and was hired to work in this capacity to help his new community support people in recovery. After starting his work in this position, he discovered he loves working with people who need his help, people with challenges that he understands very well. He is rewarded for having unusual expertise. He can be effective in ways that few others could be because of his years of lived experience, ultimately finding a sustainable path in his own recovery.

Part II

HOW NEUROSCIENCE CHANGED WHAT WE KNOW ABOUT TREATING THIS DISEASE

Chapter 12

MOTIVATED TO LEARN HOW
TO TREAT OPIOID ADDICTION

IN ABOUT 2014, WE had already seen a lot of heroin use in our town. I was working in the emergency department one night when a community college coed was brought in by her mother. The young woman had horrible abscesses on her once beautiful slender arms and her mother was, of course, very concerned. This college student was from a different community and this mother had traveled quite a distance to visit her daughter to find out why she was not doing well in school.

At her bedside the patient's mother told me that she was sleeping all the time and thought it was because of a medical condition that needed attention. She was right, it was a serious medical condition that required immediate attention to prevent sepsis and the loss of a limb, even potentially the loss of life itself. But the cause of the medical condition was not what she was expecting. The mother was peppering me with questions. My patient clearly had not informed her mother that she was dependent on black tar heroin and that the abscesses were a result of the intravenous injections of this impure drug readily available on the streets of this town. When the young woman was essentially forced by these circumstances to come to the ER for treatment I was in a difficult spot because the patient had not revealed to her mother that she was an opioid user. To protect the privacy of the young woman, I asked the mother to step out of the room for a few minutes while I spoke with the patient alone. At that point I asked if we could be honest with her mother and talk about the heroin use. She agreed that there was no benefit in denying the truth any longer. I invited her mother back in and then left the room so that this information could be shared by the patient with her mother, privately.

When I returned some minutes later to explain the needed treatment for the abscesses, the mother, in her grief, had become enraged. She demanded to know why no one had warned her that her daughter would be at great risk living in this community.

"What are you doctors doing about this?" the mother asked. "Don't you have a responsibility to inform and teach the community as well as the incoming college students about this problem? Shouldn't this town be telling parents about the unfortunate availability of illegal drugs so that they would know what their children could be exposed to while they are studying here?"

I felt terribly sad that this young woman had been caught in the web of addiction just as she began her college studies, a young adult in a town where she was far from the safety and protection of her family and friends. I knew her mother had a point. Why wasn't this subject being discussed in this community? Was I complicit with the silence?

My professional code of conduct always required that I restrain myself in conversations with my patients and their families. This case was not an exception. I could not unload on this mother for my own benefit and tell her that I had experienced what I also felt was an inappropriate silence when I moved into this community.

My high school-aged son Bezzy had joined me in this community soon after Lee and I moved into town. No one I spoke to before his arrival had told me about the pervasive street drugs, to warn me about a problem that I would need to fully understand to protect my young son. Instead, the subject was avoided, and in retrospect, that spoke volumes about the unwillingness of the community to come to terms with its dark secret. I discovered too late the denial of the drug abuse problem from every authority figure in town. Unfortunately for my son and myself, we were forced to learn about this life-altering disease the hard way.

However, what I recognized after listening to this mother was that I had to do something to change the trajectory of this disease in this town. By that time my own son had also been trapped by opioid use and although I could not bring in my own personal experiences for discussion, her questions pushed me to consider further what we physicians and community leaders should do to prevent this disease and how we could treat the disease of OUD most effectively.

As an outsider living in this town for about four years at that time, I already realized that my realm of influence was limited. My activities and involvements would be restricted to medical problems. Most difficult for me was finding an effective strategy to treat opioid use disorder and to counter its associated stigma. What I already understood about the stigma experienced by those afflicted and by extension, courtesy stigma of those who loved them and wanted to help, is a common negative perception that Bez had described to me when he was in recovery.

It is a mantra used as an excuse to not help, "Once an addict, always an addict."

Perhaps the hesitation to help is that for a long time there was no known successful treatment for this disease. Sadly, even my profession had perpetuated this outdated view that extended for years beyond the discovery of a medication that was effective in treating opioid addiction and could already have been saving lives.

Chapter 13

UNDERSTANDING THE SCIENCE
OF OPIOID ADDICTION

THANKS TO THE PROGRESS of neuroscience research and a lot more awareness of the stigma associated with this disease, medical providers now have
the information that enables us to effectively treat this disease. Why it took
so long for this easy-to-use, inexpensive medication to receive its deserved
recognition and acceptance as a treatment for OUD is still puzzling to most
of us.

Complex barriers blamed for the lack of access to this effective treatment should be recognized. Some have speculated that this treatment is not
particularly profitable for anyone and perhaps that is why it has not been
marketed in the traditional American way. Ryan Hampton wrote *American
fix: Inside the Opioid Addiction Crisis–and How to End It* which was published in 2018. He has been an advocate for change at every level of our
society to prevent deaths from opioid use disorder.

He stated, "Access to good programs, especially for people who are
experiencing intense need, is critical." [1]

He goes further by quoting Carol McDaid, cofounder of the McShin
Foundation who emphasized that having immediate help is key. "When
people with substance use disorders express a willingness to get help, there
is a very short window of opportunity. This window can close very quickly,
so it is crucial that services are available the same day the individual ex-
presses a willingness." In other words, requiring people in withdrawal due

---

1. Hampton, *American Fix*, 223–31.

to OUD to wait an extra hour, an extra day, or another week to get the medication they must have to recover is neither realistic nor humane.

There has also been criticism for detox and drug rehab programs for using methods that are based on the 12-Step Program, a traditional support for people with alcoholism. Research has found that its effectiveness in treating opioid use disorder is low. Research data shows that outcomes after treating the disease of OUD with buprenorphine/naloxone is significantly better than with the 12-Step approach alone. So why has medication assisted treatment been poorly accepted by the rehab facilities?

One unfortunate possibility is that operators of treatment facilities knew that those struggling with recovery would have to return again and again for the counseling-based treatment of opioid addiction when it was not combined with the one medication that could permanently change lives. Not providing the needed medication that could effectively treat the disease would guarantee return customers. This seems harsh but there was a potential profit-motive for their downplaying the importance of buprenorphine in the treatment of opioid use disorder.

According to an opinion published December 13, 2023 in the New York Times, Dr. Frank of the National Institutes of Health was quoted as saying, "What you had were mom-and-pop franchises. They didn't get much money or support, but they also weren't held to any real standards." Then he goes on to add, "As a result, the 12-Step method tends to prevail – but while Alcoholics Anonymous and Narcotics Anonymous have helped millions of people, they have also been known to actively discourage the use of lifesaving anti-addictions medications." And . . ."It's a bit like the Wild West out there. They're doing things that are not only not evidence-based but that are actively opposed to the evidence."[2]

My own physician peers who should have been more analytical and critical of this counseling-only method in those early years did nothing of significance to oppose this ineffective method that should have been stopped.

I have encountered some people with opioid use disorder who say they have found traditional in-patient treatments to be lifesaving. In many more cases, however, people in recovery have gone into in-patient rehab seven or eight times without ever finding resolution. Counseling alone is ineffective for many, and most people can't afford repeated admissions

2. Interlandi, *48 Million Americans,* https://www.nytimes.com/2023/12/13/opinion/addiction-policy-treatment-opioid.html.

anyway. Medicaid traditionally wouldn't pay for it, and in my son's experience, even private insurance would pay only a portion with the patient and/or family members shelling out considerable sums of money. For that reason, most people who were attempting to achieve sobriety wouldn't have the chance to undergo this expensive in-patient treatment. As it turns out there is consistent evidence-based research that demonstrates a better way to help people struggling with opioid recovery.

Outcomes based research is the gold standard for accepted medical treatments for every disease. This means that diseases are studied using research methods that allow various treatments for a particular disease to be compared without allowing subjective bias, and to rank their respective levels of effectiveness. In the case of opioid use disorder there was progress in neuroscience research twenty-five years ago that discovered the benefits of buprenorphine for this population. Really shocking is how long it has taken for its current level of acceptance by the medical establishment in this country. Libby Jones, Director of Overdose Prevention at the Global Health Advocacy Incubator, reported at the National Overdose Prevention Leadership Summit (virtual) on November 16, 2023 that only 7–10 percent of American medical providers were able to prescribe buprenorphine before the MAT Act was passed in December of 2022. When this law came into effect all medical providers with a Drug Enforcement Administration (DEA) registration were then allowed to prescribe buprenorphine. In addition, a new federal law enacted in 2024 has permanently eliminated the requirement for an X-waiver, a major barrier for buprenorphine prescribing.[3] Now there are 1.8 million potential prescribers in the United States.

The most consistent results for treatment of opioid use disorder when a person is ready to stop using opioids to get high is a medication that was designed exclusively for this purpose. It provides the biggest treatment bang for the buck, and when an addicted person is ready to make the changes necessary, it works!

When neuroscientists started to understand the disease of opioid addiction all those years ago, buprenorphine was researched and found to have validity as a treatment medication. This drug was then approved by the United States FDA for treatment of OUD in the year 2002. Eventually, in 2016, the laws for prescribing this medication changed so that primary care providers and emergency medicine physicians could become involved in providing care for people with this stigmatized medical diagnosis when

---

3. SAMHSA, *Medication for Treatment,* https://federalregister.gov/d/2024-01693.

previously only addiction specialists were allowed this privilege. Unlike methadone that by law had only been routinely dispensed in-person daily and not prescribed, the drug buprenorphine when combined with naloxone could be prescribed for weeks or even a month at a time, depending on the progress of the person in recovery. The ingredient, naloxone, is blended with buprenorphine when formulated in a film or tablet form to prevent this medication from being injected intravenously. This combination is available generically, however is also well known by the brand name Suboxone. The addition of naloxone to buprenorphine is what reduces its potential for diversion and abuse.

Most patients eventually can get a prescription for a refillable 30-day supply when the disease is stable. It comes in a variety of doses, depending on the needs of the individual and is determined by a trial period at the time of induction which is when the patient is started on this medication. As the person in recovery is monitored by an out-patient medical provider, the dose and frequency will continue to be adjusted as needed to meet the requirements of the patient who can then be functioning normally in society.

According to physicians who provide inductions for patients in their ER's, the initial dose for buprenorphine has gone up since fentanyl became the predominant opioid available on the streets in recent years. It is no longer heroin; often it is a mixture of opioids and fentanyl is usually present.[4] The way that buprenorphine works is that this treatment drug has the highest affinity for neurological receptors of all the opioids including morphine, heroin, and fentanyl. Buprenorphine can displace all the other opioid drugs in a person's system. That means the buprenorphine attaches to the opioid receptors, preventing other opioids from having access to them.

As a result of a property called lipophilicity (adipose or fat tissue loving), the opioids including fentanyl do not leave the body quickly, they just leave the brain. As a result, tolerance is deep. That means, although the brain of the person who uses opioids thinks the opioid is gone, it isn't. It has only been moved into the body's fatty tissues. To achieve a perceptible high, a person using opioids is, over time, able to metabolize a higher dose of the opioid drug without overdosing. The more concentrated the opioid drug being used, the more buprenorphine it will take to displace all the opioids stored in the adipose tissue.

4. Nelson, *Challenges and Understanding*, NOPL Summit virtual presentation.

Also, over time when a person is prevented from using opioids in a context such as jail, prison or in-patient rehab, tolerance decreases. This means that a person who hasn't used opioids for several weeks, months or years, upon using again can die of an overdose when taking a relatively low dose compared to prior self-dosing habits.

There are many benefits to be had from buprenorphine. Among the most important is the freedom it provides from the constant craving and distraction of the addiction. Being treated with Suboxone makes it possible to work, to have normal family relationships, to be a good parent, to go to school to receive the benefits of trade or professional advancement and to become a respected member of the community again. Like anyone else with a medical diagnosis, opioid use disorder should be treated in a HIPPA compliant way that allows people to have their privacy allowing them to keep their medical condition confidential.

This treatment is now the standard of care for people who are ready to quit using opioids and want to resume having a normal life. This medication may be necessary for the rest of a person's life or if able to wean off the buprenorphine, it could be used again later in recovery when a person experiences triggers and is struggling to avoid a return to the use of opioids.

In the United States we already know there are millions of people who have been exposed to opioids at levels that predispose them to having a return of the craving later when they have been opioid-free for a long time. To make a treatment medication available to all those with this disease at any time, to prevent them from giving in to a strong craving that could lead them to take a potentially deadly dose of an opioid like fentanyl from the street, we must find ways to make this medication available everywhere to prevent unnecessary deaths.

What I propose, in alignment with many emergency physicians all over this country, is that emergency departments consistently become a place where buprenorphine is available as an initial treatment through the process that is called induction. A recent study published January 29, 2024 by *JAMA Network Open* titled "Emergency Department Access to Buprenorphine for Opioid Use Disorder" found that among patients with OUD presenting to emergency departments, implementing low-threshold access to medications for OUD was associated with a substantially higher likelihood of follow-up treatment engagement 1 month later. In this study of 464 patients with OUD, 86 percent received buprenorphine treatment in the ER and 50 percent remained engaged in OUD treatment one month later, compared with 23 percent who did not receive ER buprenorphine treatment.[5]

The other option has been out-patient clinics providing patients with a prescription and giving the opioid user instructions on how to start the buprenorphine/naloxone on their own at home when they are in full withdrawal. According to the recent data, the adherence to the treatment may not be as high as when emergency departments provide the induction.

An even newer approach in Camden, New Jersey involving the EMS Fellowship at Cooper University Hospital was described during a presentation by Gerard Carroll, MD, Addiction Medicine Specialist at the virtual National Overdose Prevention Leadership Summit in November, 2023. He reported that sometimes an ambulance is the opioid user's only access to care. These people with OUD are evaluated according to a protocol and treated with buprenorphine/naloxone in the ambulance by the EMT and invited to this hospital's walk-in clinic after the induction. These patients do not require an appointment at the out-patient clinic where they are invited for follow-up to obtain their future prescriptions for Suboxone. The results of more than 300 field inductions completed to date included the following: a warning must be provided to all patients treated with buprenorphine that it cannot be taken with methadone. Among their treated patients there was no evidence of precipitated withdrawal, an estimated half of these patients refused to be transported to the ER, and on-scene time by the ambulance crew only increased seven minutes. Also encouraging was the finding that 67 percent of those inducted in the ambulance attended their first appointment in the clinic and after 30 days 75 percent were still participating. Also important to the longevity of the program, was improved job satisfaction among the EMT's, and other support staff associated with this effective approach to beginning MAT for people with OUD.[6]

Buprenorphine/naloxone cannot be given successfully when an opioid user is not in withdrawal because it will act as an antidote to the opioid. As discussed above, the opioids that a person has in their system will be displaced by the buprenorphine and this sudden reduction of the effects of the opioid drug will put that person into sudden unpleasant withdrawal. That person will not have a good first experience with buprenorphine and so this should be avoided.

5. Herring and Rosen, *ED Access to Buprenorphine*, JAMA Network.

6. Carroll, *Emergency Response to Overdose*, NOPL Summit virtual presentation.

Before prescribing Suboxone, a scoring system is used by medical teams to evaluate a patient's severity of withdrawal, which an opioid user will usually experience within twelve to thirty-six hours after last use. There are at least two brands of buprenorphine/naloxone available in the United States; most often used are Suboxone and Zubsolv. These drugs as well as their generic forms are not equivalent to each other so it's important for medical providers to be familiar with the specific drug being prescribed. These are opioid medications controlled by the Drug Enforcement Agency (DEA) on Schedule III. Their only legal use is to control the primitive functions of the brain to prevent the cravings and behaviors that make life difficult for an addicted person. These drugs can also be used to help a user of prescription opioid medications be treated for severe withdrawal when dependence occurs after long periods of using opioids to treat pain. People will usually need to take this medication for many months, years or permanently to treat their disease successfully. There should not be any stigma associated with using these medications to treat this disorder because this is a disease not unlike diabetes or hypertension in terms of their probable need for medications daily on a permanent basis to prevent death.

So, again about naloxone—it is an ingredient added to buprenorphine in several different brands and it is also available as a generic drug in the same combination. This formulation of buprenorphine with naloxone prevents people from crushing the tablets and dissolving them for intravenous injection or dissolving the soluble film for injection. Naloxone has little bioavailability when used sublingually which prevents it from affecting the metabolism of buprenorphine when used orally, but when administered intravenously it will cause withdrawal. Thus, this second medication is added to the buprenorphine to help to prevent its use as an IV drug thus reducing its appeal for people actively using opioids to achieve euphoria, also known as a high.

One of the new developments in certain parts of the country is the arrival of xylazine as an additive in many illegal drugs sold on the streets. William J. Lynch, PharmD, provided an update for the virtual audience attending the National Overdose Prevention Leadership Summit in November, 2023.[7] Xylazine is an alpha-2 agonist only legally used in this country to sedate large animals. It has never been approved for human consumption. The danger is that many people using illegal drugs are not aware that there is xylazine in the fentanyl/heroin/cocaine or meth they are using. It

7. Lynch, Xylazine—*What Is Happening Now*, NOPL Summit virtual presentation.

produces somnolence that lasts up to five hours and it increases the risk for respiratory depression. The only way we can treat xylazine in an overdose situation is to provide a naloxone drip for a very long time. Sometimes intubation is required because its sedative effect is so severe. Another serious potential problem with xylazine is that it causes a reduced heart rate and thus circulation to the extremities is compromised, causing ulcerations of the skin, usually in the extremities. Individuals with these skin wounds can require skin grafts or even amputations when the wounds become severely infected. In most cases the necrosis of the skin occurs at injection sites of the drugs containing xylazine.

In addition to naloxone to maintain normal respirations for patients fighting the effects of xylazine, clonidine and tizanidine can be given to reduce the effects of withdrawal. A patient who has overdosed with xylazine present in the drugs used will have fixed pin-point pupils. Airway protection is important due to the severe sedation seen with this type of overdose. Atropine can be used to treat a low heart rate. When a person must be intubated, the sedation medication of choice for this type of overdose is Precedex (dexmedetomidine).

Chapter 14

THE COLORADO HOSPITAL ASSOCIATION STARTS AN OPIOID ADDICTIONS TREATMENT MOVEMENT

AFTER WORKING IN MY community for several years observing the worsening of the opioid epidemic, also observing increasing numbers of overdoses along with many deaths, the beginning of hope arrived in our region in November of 2017. A physician invited all the medical providers in our county to a lunch presentation titled, "The Opioid Epidemic." As a representative of the Colorado Hospital Association (CHA), Dr. Don Stader presented data from our state alongside national data on the epidemic.

In 2015, 33,091 deaths in the nation were from prescription opioids and heroin overdoses. In 2016, that number almost doubled to an estimated 63,000 opioid related deaths. In Colorado that year, 912 people died from overdosing, of which 504 involved opioids. He emphasized that the deaths that occur are just the tip of the iceberg, and we need to recognize that for every 1 death there are 10 addiction treatment program admissions for substance abuse, 32 ER visits for misuse or abuse, and 130 people who are either abusing or dependent on opioids.

This physician then provided a lesson in neuroscience, teaching us that addiction to opioids results in a reward system malfunction due to endorphins, dynorphins and dopamine flooding the neural synapses at a level high enough to cause brain failure. When opioid use begins, either because of a prescription to treat pain or because of a single bad decision to try an extremely addictive drug, the result at first is a high. After that first dopamine elevation, the user may find it necessary to take the drug time and time again to feel normal and to avoid withdrawal. When it progresses to this level of use, it is a medical disease, and drug-seeking is compulsive and difficult to control. The consequences of obtaining the drug becomes less important than the desire to avoid withdrawal.

At that point, he proposed, on behalf of the CHA and the American College of Emergency Physicians, a four-step solution to address the opioid epidemic:

1. Limiting the use of opioids in the emergency room

2. Selecting Alternatives to Opioids (ALTO) for painful conditions

3. Induction of opioid-dependent patients who are seeking sobriety along with a referral to Medication Assisted Treatment (MAT) outpatient clinics for long-term support

4. Community program development to promote Harm Reduction, which is a way of keeping people with opioid addiction as safe as possible until they are ready to stop using opioids to get high

The data he presented was supplemented by a study from the Centers for Disease Control and Prevention (CDC) Morbidity and Mortality Weekly Report (MMWR), *Characteristics of Initial Episodes and Likelihood of Long-Term Opioid Use - United States, 2006–2015; March 17, 2017/66(10):* 65–269. This study found that the number of days' supply of the first opioid prescription strongly correlated with increases in the probability of continuing use of opioids. As a result, acute pain should be treated with twenty pills maximum, although fewer pills are better, and ten pills is best. Post-surgical pain should be treated with only five days of opioid medications, seven days is the maximum.

Chapter 15

OPIOID ADDICTIONS TREATMENT
COMES TO MY HOSPITAL IN STAGES

FEELING THE URGENCY OF sharing this information, I discussed with our hospital's administration the steps I felt we should take to make changes needed in our ER. I presented to our hospital's Board of Directors the proposals for change that I felt sure would make a difference in our community relative to the epidemic in our county. I suggested starting ALTO and MAT programs in our ER as well as in the Rural Health out-patient clinic and I urged including the entire hospital. I begged for permission to work with our county's health department on Harm Reduction measures in the community such as making naloxone available in all the ambulances and police cars as well as approval to explore other needed measures. To start saving lives immediately, we all needed to encourage families and friends of people with opioid addiction to learn how to administer this opioid reversal medication. The data from the Colorado Department of Public Health and Environment was compelling.

I received the go-ahead to work with our ER physicians on decreasing their opioid prescribing, and the hospital's Board also supported teaching physicians the alternatives to opioid administration while these patients were in the ER. But MAT and Harm Reduction did not get the green light at that time.

Alternatives to opioids had to be rediscovered by physicians and APP's who were trained and had only worked in the era of limitless narcotics for the treatment of pain. As a result of deliberately moving away from opioids to treat chronic and even acute pain, there are now a multitude of new medications and treatments listed for us by the experts that are useful to manage pain. They include ketamine, Toradol, Haldol, gabapentin, lidocaine trigger-point injections, capsaicin cream for topical application, physical therapy, and TENS units as well as dry needling administered by physical therapists that can help many patients. There is also comprehensive behavioral therapy (CBT) by Behavioral Health professionals. There are others I have not yet been trained to use or haven't had access to and they are reported to include IV Tylenol (expensive), lidocaine drips, desmopressin, nitrous oxide, nerve blocks and acupuncture, and without doubt there will be many more to come. Other physicians have already received this training to be consistent with standards of care in their specialties, to the benefit of their patients.

A lot of talking with our patients to re-educate them about pain management also had to occur in the years that followed. The patients' expectations about what medical providers could do for chronic pain had to change as well. It was a challenge for all concerned. Some medical providers working in the ER refused to change their prescribing practices and ultimately were terminated from our hospital Emergency Department's physician team. Like any other professional group, change does not come easily and sometimes educating and using reason just isn't possible to effect an urgent necessary change.

Annually I attended the Colorado Hospital Association's (CHA) Opioid Summits, and those of us representing our hospital received step-by-step guidance on what to do next as a member hospital. In 2019 we received the CHA's encouragement and specific steps were provided to initiate a Suboxone induction program in the ER. The snag in our community was that we didn't have any out-patient clinic willing to start prescribing buprenorphine/naloxone, which meant that the patients we inducted on Suboxone in the ER would not have anywhere to go to continue their regular clinic visits to receive prescriptions. The closest clinic was two hours away, which is too far to expect anyone to travel for what would start out as weekly appointments for their care. Their out-patient support would have to consist of counseling, medical evaluations regularly along with drug testing, written prescriptions and other services when needed.

That led to many formal and informal discussions between all the community stakeholders actively providing care for people with OUD, including the county health department, primary care providers, mental health professionals and an addictions services clinic that had started operating in our location but was dispensing only methadone, not Suboxone.

Yes, we had made progress, but we still didn't have a seamless wraparound treatment plan in place for people in our community who had already developed this disease. Instead of waiting for movement on the out-patient clinic side, I realized that we had work to do in the ER and that was an area I could influence directly.

None of our ER physicians were X-waivered which was the special Drug Enforcement Agency (DEA) training prerequisite for prescribing Suboxone at that time. That had to be the next step. I obtained my X-waiver training in September of 2019 and as the Medical Director, I started gently pushing the ER physicians at our hospital to get theirs too. By May of 2020, four of the 10 practicing physicians in our ER were X-waivered. These four had been won over by the information they had received through this training about the importance of MAT inductions to be available in the ER for a community like ours. They were eager to get started and they supported my efforts to add MAT to the treatments we could offer our community from the ER. This was a turning point as the physicians I worked with saw this medication as the practical solution to a deadly disease we were not previously able to impact with a positive outcomes-based treatment.

Fortunately, several years later the laws for the DEA changed to eliminate the separate certification needed by medical providers so that the X-waiver was no longer a requirement for prescribing buprenorphine. Any medical provider with a DEA registration was then able and is now able to prescribe buprenorphine/naloxone to treat OUD.

I used the information from the CHA and prepared our ER for the addition of MAT services as a matter of medical necessity. Our RN Clinical Manager Leslie Day supported the addition of Suboxone to the hospital's formulary, having seen the need firsthand. The two of us, feet on the ground in this ER daily, kept going despite increasingly negative comments we were receiving from certain members of the nursing and pharmacy staff. Several threatened to quit before they would help provide MAT for a patient trying to recover from opioid addiction. They apparently envisioned a long line of opioid users at the door who would derail emergent care we could provide for others. Of course, that was not what occurred when we went live with MAT in our hospital.

By the time the two of us went to the CHA Opioid Summit in February of 2020, accompanied by a member of our hospital's C-suite, I was aware that stigma against people with addictions was alive and well even within our hospital walls. Contrary to the negative attitudes of these people who feared what they did not understand, studies have shown that 61 percent of people treated with MAT succeed with getting their normal lives back. This is so incredible when before this the recovery rates were terribly low. It was imperative that we begin to treat this addiction as a disease that merited outcomes-based treatment like all the other diseases that we were treating. We now had a treatment to offer our community that was backed by scientific research, and we were determined to teach those who were not yet convinced that this was the right thing to do.

I presented a 4-minute video from PBS, "The View from Here: Shelly Elkington/Fierce Advocacy",[1] to the hospital's administrative team. It was designed to be an eye-opener to teach non-medical people about the disease of opioid use disorder. A mother talks about losing her daughter to opioids because of the stigma she had internalized about having this disease. Her daughter would not ask for help because she was afraid of the stigma she expected to encounter. Stigma destroys lives. Stigma kills.

My message was that the senseless destruction of lives must stop. After viewing this video, the assembled administrators recognized that our hospital still had a lot of work to do to remove the barriers to treatment that came in the form of stigma. Leslie and I gained some important ground with that presentation. But we needed to continue addressing this issue with staff in the ER, in our pharmacy, and in all the corners of the hospital. This work had to be done for the well-being of not just these patients with this disease but also for the well-being of the whole community.

By this time, I had decided to stop asking for permission from everyone to proceed with the steps needed to put this policy and its new procedures in place. I knew we were not going to have consensus among all the clinical team members, and we couldn't wait for everyone to agree to this change before we started implementing the new treatment. The individuals who needed to be aware were already involved. They were given opportunities to have input as we developed the plan. The others who were trying to sabotage the plans were attempting to manipulate their supervisors with whatever power they felt they could wield. This came in the form of emotional threats that they would quit and take all their peers with them. Additionally, nasty and unprofessional comments were being thrown around as a means of attempting influence. It seemed like the few who were strongly

1. Elkington, *Fierce Advocacy,* PBS Denver.

opposed thought they could go on strike and force the hospital's Board of Directors to stop this effort to bring Suboxone to our hospital. Their efforts ultimately failed.

When the ER received its first patient requiring Suboxone treatment after it was placed in our dispensing unit, a nurse with whom I worked refused to administer the medication I had ordered for this patient's withdrawal. It was a tiny film that was dissolvable, and it just required being placed inside the mouth for the patient to absorb the medication through the mucus membrane. One or two minutes of observation was needed after its placement to make sure the patient had left it alone where it had been placed. I asked why she would not place the medication on the side of the cheek or under the tongue as I described, and she reported she required more training and could not follow my instructions. Thus, I administered the Suboxone film myself inside the cheek of that patient. This resulted in a most grateful response from the patient when he found relief from his withdrawal symptoms about twenty minutes later. He was discharged home with a prescription that he would get filled at a pharmacy.

That patient had a family member who called to speak with me later that evening when his cousin had been discharged from the ER, thanking me for saving him from suicide. That, to me, confirmed the urgency that existed to help those who were desperate for relief from their addiction. We could not be deterred in our work to save these lives.

The experience I had with the first nurse who was asked to administer Suboxone soon led to a mandatory training session by the ER Nurse Manager where all the nurses were required to complete the in-service. Gradually each nurse experienced the wonderful results that induction with Suboxone could provide for the patients who needed this treatment. It couldn't be denied that this medication was a game changer in our community. However, these inductions didn't begin until we had developed a memorandum of understanding with a clinic willing to treat them as out-patients long term. After receiving an initial dose of Suboxone plus a prescription to last them a few days, they would need to be seen in the out-patient setting before they ran out of their medication.[2]

Fortunately, our community's hospital now had a CEO who had grown up in this region. She was fearless and she had a heart for service. She had demonstrated her abilities as a leader in her early management of the Covid-19 epidemic when new safety measures for our staff and our

2. *Initiating Buprenorphine Treatment in the ED*, NIDA.nih.gov.

patients had to be implemented. When our progress in starting Suboxone in the ER stalled because of the lack of a local out-patient clinic to partner with us in treating this disease, I enlisted her help. Together we composed a letter that was sent to the leadership of the existing addictions out-patient treatment facility in our town. She asked the clinic to add Suboxone to their list of approved medications rather than prescribing only methadone for the long-term care of people with opioid use disorder.

After a nail-biting delay of six weeks we received an affirmative answer. At that point what remained was working out the specific protocol of the partnership between our hospital and the out-patient addictions treatment center. With this last hurdle cleared, we were finally prepared to care for the people of this region who were struggling with OUD. This partnership would provide state-of-the-art Medication Assisted Treatment services complete with the physician, behavioral health therapist, nursing staff and the social worker to provide appropriate care for this population group. The final step was approval from our hospital's Board of Directors. This occurred on July 22, 2020. We had the go-ahead we needed, and the MAT protocol was implemented after specific details of our cooperative process was completed.

What surprised me more than anything was the benefit that our work for the Emergency Department provided the whole hospital. No sooner had we started treating patients in the ER with Suboxone than a nurse from the obstetrics floor came to the ER physician's workroom to speak with me. She asked if I could help treat a mother who had just given birth who was in full opioid withdrawal. The new mother was likely going to leave the hospital without her newborn if we could not offer a treatment with Suboxone.

Of course I said, "Yes, I can help."

I called the obstetrician who said she had no experience prescribing Suboxone and didn't know what to do next. I provided her and the nursing staff on the OB Unit with the protocol we were using in the ER and taught them all how to use this medication.

In turn, I learned from the obstetrics team that the first benefit of keeping the mothers with their newborns in the hospital after receiving treatment with Suboxone was that it would allow them to continue their parental custody. Since the hospital was required by law to report the mothers who were active opioid users, these addicted mothers and their infants were normally separated at birth with the infant being placed in a foster home until the mother could demonstrate her sobriety to the satisfaction of the court of law. Suboxone treatment would enable these mothers to parent their own children from the beginning of their children's lives. Social workers from Child Protective Services were required to follow them to make sure the infants were receiving appropriate care and that the parents were continuing with their own treatment for OUD. Avoiding the separation of infant and mother at birth is so important to keep the family intact, thereby encouraging the mother and often the father as well, to pursue a life of sobriety. This healing for the benefit of a young family is made possible by the induction of the mother with Suboxone in the hospital setting.

And what is the effect of Suboxone during pregnancy? Recently another study was reported in the *New England Journal of Medicine* that demonstrated that Suboxone is safer for the mother and the fetus than the alternative, methadone.[3]

In the end it comes down to following the science of outcomes-based research for opioid treatment. The disease of opioid use disorder can be conquered. Joyful life resumes and functional relationships are again possible.

3. Suarez et al., *Buprenorphine versus Methadone in Pregnancy*, 2033–44.

Chapter 16

HARM REDUCTION IS HOW WE CARE FOR PEOPLE WITH OPIOID ADDICTION BEFORE TREATMENT

GETTING SUBOXONE STARTED IN our hospital was a major victory but in the step-by-step process of the CHA, we still had the last recommendation to consider. It was possibly the most controversial and therefore the hardest of all to sell to those not yet understanding this disease. Harm Reduction is what it is called, and this group of interventions includes all the ways that have been developed to support people in active use of opioids before they are ready for sobriety.

The risk of contracting life-threatening infections such as HIV and hepatitis as well as injection site infections from IV drug use can lead to the loss of limbs in addition to deadly sepsis. These harms can be reduced with needle exchange programs and regular lab work to determine exposure to deadly diseases.

When overdose occurs, Narcan kits enable friends, family and even strangers on the street to save lives when people accidentally overdose or when they are losing hope and deliberately overdose. The contact with a human being who cares enough about them to save their life can make all the difference.

The bottom line is that Harm Reduction keeps the user of opioids alive and helps to reduce their risk of health problems that will prevent them from having a normal life when they are ready for sobriety. These measures not only reduce the risk to the person with the addiction, but it also reduces the actual financial cost of recovery from OUD that we all support with our health insurance and government programs. Preventing this loss is not only the compassionate thing to do but this also is the smart thing to do as a nation. The cost to society is lower when these additional diseases and disabilities can be prevented. As a society we need to save these lives because they are our future employees and contributors of good works in our communities.

The Health Department in Prowers County began dispensing Narcan kits with the simple training that is required to administer this life-saving medication for someone who is unarousable after using an opioid. Every county in this country should be able to provide this medication (for free) for anyone who requests access to this drug. This is Harm Reduction at its most basic level.

The consequences of social separation due to Covid-19 had made this disease even more deadly for this population. It appears that the numbers of deaths from OUD increased during 2020 because these people were using opioid drugs alone instead of in groups which had normally been the practice. The stigma of this disease was already forcing those with opioid use disorder to isolate and Covid-19 increased that removal from their communities.

There are test strips now available for drug users to test their illegal drug of choice to find out if it contains fentanyl before they use it. This enables them to protect themselves better against accidental overdose. If they know there is fentanyl in the drug they are using, such as cocaine, methamphetamine, or illegally marketed marijuana, it allows the user to avoid this deadly drug. It can save lives by preventing a potential user from being poisoned with fentanyl.

More innovative programs are immerging throughout this country as the urgency to prevent deaths increases. As a result of the National Overdose Prevention Leadership Summit (free virtual event) to which I was invited to participate on November 16–17, 2023, the work of several organizations was discussed. Their websites will be included here for the readers' use:

- https://BridgetoTreatment.org

  This is the website for CA Bridge, based in Oakland, California. Network for Emergency Addiction Treatment (NEAT) is one branch of this national out-reach program. An ER can use the Guidelines provided in the BUP Quick Start protocol

- https://www.advocacyincubator.org

Overdose prevention – Global Health Advocacy Incubator

- https://COCHS.org

  Health Care Initiatives for Justice-Involved Populations at Community Oriented Correctional Health Services.

Chapter 17

SUBOXONE TREATMENT
AND CORRECTIONAL FACILITIES

MANY COUNTY JAILS STILL do not provide Suboxone for inmates who are in opioid withdrawal after being incarcerated. Traditionally, there has been no treatment for opioid use disorder while serving their sentences. Unfortunately, without this medication these inmates are destined to be at high risk for overdose when they are released from jail. The physiology that causes a person to become tolerant of ever-increasing doses of opioids dramatically raises their risk of taking an overdose accidentally when they have access to opioids after release. These opioid users may even be aware of this and try to self-administer a low dose to accommodate a period of abstinence. If they have not used opioids for a period of weeks, months or longer, they will not be capable of surviving the dose they had easily tolerated previously. And now with fentanyl present in most illegal drugs, the risk is higher than ever of accidentally receiving opioids in a mix of illegal drugs. This can cause an accidental overdose and death will result unless someone has Narcan and administers this antidote within minutes. Many inmates released after incarceration have died because of this miscalculation of potential risk.

Ideally, anyone who is using opioids at the time of arrest should be inducted with Suboxone when they are in withdrawal after arriving in jail. This inmate should continue to be treated with Suboxone while incarcerated. When released from jail, that person should get an appointment with a clinic that will prescribe this life-saving medication after their release without having a gap in their MAT to prevent a relapse of opioid use.

Vivitrol is another medication that can be given to inmates but it is contraindicated in pregnant women, whereas Suboxone is safe, as discussed earlier. Suboxone also helps a pregnant woman struggling with opioid use disorder transition into a life of sobriety before the baby arrives or even after the newborn arrives so that she can continue to provide care for her infant after birth. She can then be mother to her own child, a priceless advantage to that child and to the community where they live.

Sam Quinones, a journalist who reported how the opioid epidemic began with his book *Dreamland* published in 2015, has recently written *The Least of Us,* a continuation of his stories with the subtitle, *True Tales of America and Hope in the Time of Fentanyl and Meth.*[1] This newer book gives examples of county jails realizing their opportunity to change lives while inmates are incarcerated. Quinones focuses on Kenton County where drug treatment programs are offered to inmates who choose to participate. They are offered support with MAT, group counseling, and the inmates' families are invited to attend classes with them while they serve time in jail. The inmates who are in recovery are held in areas that are separated from the non-participating inmates. As the inmates in recovery prepare to complete their sentences, there are opportunities for them to be educated for the workforce and to become employed upon their release. This is a program that works for the benefit of the whole community.

1. Quinones, *The Least of Us,* 254–57.

Chapter 18

COMPLETING THE SUPPORT SYSTEMS NEEDED
WITHIN COMMUNITIES FOR PEOPLE IN RECOVERY

HARM REDUCTION, IN SOME of its applications, is controversial because it is commonly thought to encourage drug addiction. Those who have experienced OUD would disagree with that stigmatic assumption. Since the medical community is becoming interested in providing the right support for these individuals to enable a full recovery, it is essential to protect their future health in advance of their receiving successful treatment some day when they are ready.

Many urban communities already offer needle exchange programs as well as disease screening to allow opioid users to receive treatment when they are found positive for HIV, hepatitis C and other blood borne diseases. This kind of proactive harm reduction can dramatically decrease the costs for taxpayers and their communities if the treatment of these diseases can be avoided or treated early, if transmission can be prevented and, additionally, save these individuals for later productive and healthy normal lives.

One of the most impossible ways to support people with OUD currently is to provide them with a safe space to inject their opioid drugs. Although a good idea in theory, it is not legal in this country in any community. This idea is becoming even more important now in urban areas where the illegally manufactured fentanyl and car-fentanyl is flooding the streets. Its high potency and inconsistent concentration are causing more deaths than ever from accidental opioid overdosing. The advantage of these safe spaces for injecting these increasingly dangerous drugs is that staff can be present and armed with Narcan. The overdoses will be reversed, using as many doses as is needed to keep the person breathing until the ambulance arrives. This essential lifesaving action can prevent overdose deaths. These staff can also make sure that the person experiencing the overdose will be transferred to an ER for completion of the care and education needed before they are discharged home.

Referral to MAT services offered at out-patient clinics for long-term prescription access as well as other organizations with whom they can develop relationships are valuable as patients recovering will need their help. The knowledgeable staff and volunteers who assist in getting people with histories of OUD back to normal living is necessary to remove barriers that are common for people desiring to re-enter normal productive society.

Sobriety housing that will allow people in recovery to live in safety and accountability while they gain their strength and ability to function again is a critical support for people in recovery.

They also require advocates to find jobs in the community. It really shouldn't take going to jail before people who want to recover from OUD can get access to the services they need for recovery.

In January of 2020, Iowa State University Sociology and Criminal Justice Professor Andrew Hochstetler presented research data at our local county health department.[1] How did this surprising contact with a university not even located in Colorado come about? Professor Hochstetler explained that he came to our county to talk to anyone who would listen. According to the data, in 2017 there were 8 overdose deaths in our county according to the CDC. Five were non-opioid overdoses. Three were opioid deaths from heroin. This was unusual for rural areas in most parts of the nation at that time.

He went on to say, "A very complete kitchen-sink predictive model predicted zero deaths in this county using the national data."

"With a small population denominator, the rate is high at 21.3 per 100,000."

What he had hoped to achieve with his presentation, was a chance to give rural leaders in this region an opportunity to talk to the government, and to provide examples of real-life cases that would give voice to the data. An additional goal was for him to clarify his understanding of outliers and error: data problems, idiosyncratic things that cannot be modeled such as bad batches of drugs that are being distributed, and oddities as opposed to emerging trends."

---

1. Hochstetler, *Why the Concern Over Opioids,* community presentation.

I emailed several population questions to Professor Hochstetler and he replied that David Peters did the analysis that had been presented.... "The simple answer... is that your county is classified by our study as rural." This definition assisted my understanding of the information that was shared later in the presentation.

Professor David Peters also sent clarifying information explaining that the county in which I lived and worked was a heroin vulnerable community.

He continued, "Our model predicted that your county should have a heroin overdose death rate of 1.2 per 100,000 people. The actual heroin overdose death rate was 10.1 per 100,000. This showed that for some reason your community has far higher heroin deaths than it should. It is a rural and sparsely populated community, yet poverty is not that high, and incomes are decent on average. The job market is also decent. There is not a lot of overprescribing of prescription opioids currently. Disability rates are not high, and most people work in relatively safe jobs (not mining or machinery manufacturing).

Professor Hochstetler had stated in his presentation that nationwide, between 1999 and 2016, opioid overdose deaths increased by 723 percent in rural locations in the United States versus large metropolitan areas, which grew only 387 percent during the same period. Of the 355,000 total who died during that period, 117 died each day and sixty-six of all overdose deaths daily were due to opioids. There is a tremendous price paid in economic losses, calculated to be $80 billion annually in this nation because of these deaths.

The findings of this far away university are useful even now several years later since solutions can be developed, if these problems as presented by Professors Hochstetler and Peters are recognized:

- Opioid epidemics occur in an environment of a growing general drug problem. Data suggests this occurs due to either an existing addict-base conducive to this problem or due to socioeconomic conditions or in some cases, both. Opioids are the latest in a long line of drug abuse, albeit fatal.

- Opioid epidemic counties tend to be left behind places. These communities are older, less diverse and with a declining industrial base. Their community characteristics are increasingly dissimilar from the rest of the United States.

- Prescription-related epidemics occur in the small and remote places. These areas have lower population densities and greater topographic variation.

- Disability-dispensing-mortality pathway is distinctive. Populations tend to work in injury-prone industries. There is lower labor participation with less strict prescribing and dispensing practices. And significantly, there is lack of access to non-prescription pain management.

- Only prescription opioid epidemic fits the deaths of despair thesis. This is the population with the greatest drug risk, greatest economic distress, local economy dominated by declining blue-color jobs and social disorder.

What are the implications for this community in which I lived and worked? These researchers provided the following solutions that needed to be considered. And potentially these researchers recommended that all should be implemented:

A. **Prevention** –

A state's regulation of legally prescribed opioids will help but not solve the crisis because illicit opioids are used as an alternative. Illicit drug enforcement through drug intelligence and interdiction as well as border security and customs require community commitment and support.

B. **Treatment** –

The county must expand treatment for all types of drug addiction. The changes needed include:

1) Continued support for medication assisted treatment (MAT)

2) The addition of MAT in the county jail

3) Medicaid/Insurance reforms

4) Increased addiction services including plentiful and affordable sobriety housing

5) Stigma-eradication efforts with drug courts differentiated from criminal processes and this should include encouragement of family involvement

C. **Economic Development** -

Must include full-time, year-around employment that pays livable wages. If the jobs are injury prone, there need to be better Occupational Safety and Health Administration (OSHA) regulations to prevent injuries.

D. **Social Capital -**

Local agency is essential. That means the community needs to get behind the need for solutions. There needs to be a local capacity to address drug issues among community members.

What would local agency look like in the town where I lived? In my view the entire list of recommendations should be carefully examined and implemented to provide all the benefits that these suggestions would bring for the community.

Among them, the public-school district and community college could promote conversations with parents about the risks associated with drugs that are available illegally. Students of all ages should be educated about the drugs that they may encounter, and they must be taught through formal programming to build their knowledge about these dangerous drugs at every grade level to prevent ever having a first exposure to them.

County and city government needs to have frequent conversations in the community about the problems faced by law enforcement in preventing the influx of illegal drugs. The need for Harm Reduction to support the well-being of the opioid users who reside in the community also requires thoughtful attention by leaders. The participation of the community in these conversations helps them understand the priorities in the spending of public monies and helps the members of the community relate to the importance of these efforts. Enlisting the aid of educators as well as addictions specialists within the local population could promote change to support those who are recovering from substance use disorders. Community action plans can allow local ideas to become the basis for change to make the town and its people stronger as they work together.

Calling out stigma and courtesy stigma will also sensitize the community to behaviors that worsen the outcomes for those in recovery. Having intentional goals can allow progress toward better community health and well-being.

Part III

AN EMERGENCY PHYSICIAN'S GUIDE TO PROVIDING MEDICATION ASSISTED TREATMENT

Chapter 19

EMERGENCY DEPARTMENT PREPARATION
TO BEGIN BUPRENORPHINE INDUCTIONS

SEVERAL STEPS NEED TO be undertaken by the Medical Director of your Emergency Department within your hospital to prepare for this program. The following are what we did at our hospital, but this is not necessarily a prescription for what will work at your facility. Use this information together with guidance from experts in your community and references provided in the previous section of this book to help you determine each step you need to take.

1. Conference with the Director of Pharmacy to discuss the planned addition of buprenorphine to the hospital's formulary. The pharmacy will need to explore different forms of the drug, including the generic options, to decide what would be the best medication to stock for hospital-wide use on the Med-Surg unit, the OB floor, and the ED.

2. Meet with the Pharmacy and Therapeutics Committee to request approval of buprenorphine/naloxone to the formulary for use on Med-Surg unit, the OB floor and the ED.

3. Meet with the administration at your institution to explain Medication Assisted Treatment and the patient-care goals that will be met with the initiation of inductions in your hospital.

4. Promote ED physician training in the prescribing of buprenorphine/naloxone. Let the ED physicians know when this program will start so that they can obtain their own training before going live. Although

the ED physicians will be able to spearhead the effort for the whole hospital, the entire medical staff should be enrolled in an educational program to prepare for treating in-patients with this medication when indicated. A recommended source of information and training for emergency physicians is CA Bridge at www.cabridge.org. The *Emergency Medicine News* published "No Excuses for Not Prescribing Buprenorphine in the ED" in September 2023, a reference for emergency physicians regarding the status of opioid use disorder in the U.S. and the need for more access to inductions to begin treatment.[1]

5. Work with specialized nurse trainers to develop a program for emergency department nurses before going live.

6. Develop your own institution's protocol and discharge practices for this population. This section is provided with the expectation that it will be copied to the extent that is needed for others to design their own programs to fit the needs of their own institutions.

7. Make Narcan (naloxone in ready-to-use nasal spray) available for free to all the patients leaving your ED after they have undergone induction. They and their family members or friends should be instructed how to use the naloxone before they leave the ED. Many states are providing this medication through grants that are available for this purpose. Contact your county's public health department for more information.

8. Discuss this program with your institution's Compliance Office to make sure that they have a chance to check the laws in your state relating to confidentiality regarding sharing medical records.

9. Start preparing the hospital's staff in every department to view videos as mandatory training before this goes live to sensitize and help them understand the need for kindness and caring towards people who seek our assistance when they have an addiction. We need to confront stigmatizing behaviors when we observe this among our own professional groups.

10. Schedule a meeting with the clinic(s) in your community who will be accepting your patients after induction in the ED to facilitate a seamless continuity of care. Also make sure that in-patients who are

---

1. Shaw, *No Excuses*, 16–17.

treated with buprenorphine/naloxone get the referral to long-term out-patient care in your community.

11. The Case Manager for buprenorphine follow-up needs to call every patient after discharge. The risk of losing them after contact with your institution is high unless there is a development of that personal relationship. The importance of having Social Worker case managers and Peer Recovery Coaching to support people with OUD is a key component to their success. The ideal situation is to offer a patient in the ED a warm hand-off to a Peer Recovery Coach before they are discharged from the emergency department after an induction.

Chapter 20

EMERGENCY DEPARTMENT MEDICATION ASSISTED
TREATMENT ALGORITHM FOR PHYSICIANS

1. First step is to identify if a patient meets criteria for Opioid Use Disorder as a diagnosis. Use *"Questionnaire for Identification of Opioid Use Disorder based on DSM-5 for Coding" (Appendix 1).* Count the number of "yes" answers and use the scale on the form to help determine a diagnosis.

2. Then, using the following additional criteria for at-risk patients, document those relevant in the history of present illness:

   - Past or current substance abuse
   - Untreated psychiatric illness
   - Younger age
   - Risky social/family environments
   - Low-income background
   - >100 mg morphine equivalences used per day
   - Frequent Emergency Department visits and other known medical co-morbidities
   - Multiple opioids prescribed and multiple providers prescribing them in the past year

3. Search the Prescription Drug Monitoring Program (PDMP) website and document what you find.

4. Using the *"Clinical Opiate Withdrawal Scale" (COWS)* identify patients in active withdrawal (*Appendix 2*). Patients with a score of 8 or higher should be considered for induction with buprenorphine/naloxone.

5. Review the *"Emergency Department MAT Induction Algorithm"* (*Appendix 3*) as it applies to this patient. This algorithm was developed by the author for use at her hospital. Using the algorithm think through all potential complications. You may want to order labs first. Discuss your plan of care with the patient.

   - Patients in active withdrawal receive buprenorphine/naloxone in the ED with monitoring while the dose is being titrated; any physician with an active DEA number can prescribe buprenorphine in the ED or hospital setting. Standard dosing begins at 8 to 16 mg (buprenorphine) sublingually, titrated to effect with a maximum daily dose of 64 mg of buprenorphine. Watch patient in the ED for one hour for effect and side effects.

   - Patients not in active withdrawal but agreeable to start MAT are instructed to make an appointment with an out-patient clinic or wait for withdrawal symptoms to occur and return to the ED at that time since they will not be receiving medication until they are in withdrawal. [1]

6. Discuss with patient harm reduction strategies. This includes two Narcan (naloxone intranasal) kits which can be provided from the ED's supply or if needed a prescription should be provided the patient or a note upon discharge for patient to pick this up in the pharmacy when the buprenorphine prescription is filled (Medicaid provides free Narcan). Patient can also call the local public health department for a limited supply of these kits, often provided after brief training. Each patient who is treated or considered for treatment with buprenorphine should receive Narcan (naloxone) or a prescription for it.

7. A streamlined algorithm that has been developed by a nationwide not-for-profit organization (www.bridgetotreatment.org), is provided in *Appendix 4* with references.

8. Refer the patient to the out-patient clinic that will provide their long-term treatment with buprenorphine/naloxone. If possible, get an appointment for the patient before they leave the ED. If this interaction

---

1. *Buprenorphine Emergency Department Quick Start*, bridgetotreatment.org.

is not during regular business hours, ask the patient to sign a consent to share their ED report with the out-patient clinic to which the patient is being referred, so that the patient can be contacted by the clinic directly (*Appendix 5*) during business hours.

9. Patient is given Discharge Instructions (*Appendix 6*) before departure that includes the phone number for the out-patient clinic where they are being referred as well as a written plan of care for their self-care until the time of their appointment at the out-patient clinic.

   - The ED physician provides the patient with a prescription for buprenorphine as a bridge until the appointment with the out-patient clinic. *Appendix 7* provides a Sample Prescription for Buprenorphine/Naloxone.

10. Emergency department staff will need to contact the patient by phone the day after they were treated in the ED to make sure they have their appointment at the out-patient clinic and to make sure they are doing well. If the ED has a Peer Recovery Coach, it is ideal to provide a warm hand-off in the ED before the patient leaves. This enhances the relationship and increases the likelihood of success for the person in recovery.

Appendix 1

QUESTIONNAIRE FOR IDENTIFICATION OF OPIOID USE DISORDER BASED ON DSM-5 FOR CODING[1]

Ask the patient about their use of opioid drugs (designated as "X" below) in the past 12 months. Keep track of the "yes" responses to determine the severity.

1. Have you often found that when you started using X that you ended up taking more than you intended to? ( ) YES   ( ) NO

2. Have you wanted to stop or cut down using or control your use of X? ( ) YES   ( ) NO

3. Have you spent a lot of time getting X or using X? ( ) YES   ( ) NO

4. Have you had a strong desire or urge to use X? ( ) YES   ( ) NO

5. Have you missed work or school or often arrived late because you were intoxicated, high or recovering from the night before? ( ) YES ( ) NO

6. Has your use of X caused problems with other people such as with family members, friends or people at work? ( ) YES   ( ) NO

7. Have you had to give up or spend less time working, enjoying hobbies, or being with others because of your drug use? ( ) YES   ( ) NO

8. Have you ever gotten high before doing something that requires coordination or concentration like driving, boating, climbing a ladder, or operating heavy machinery? ( ) YES   ( ) NO

1. *Questionnaire for OUD Coding,* drugabuse.gov.

9. Have you continued to use even though you knew that the drug caused you problems like making you depressed, anxious, agitated, or irritable? ( ) YES ( ) NO

10. Have you found you need to use much more drug to get the same effect than you did when you first started taking it? ( ) YES ( ) NO

11. When you reduced or stopped using, did you have withdrawal symptoms or feel sick (aches, shaking, fever, weakness, diarrhea, nausea, sweating, heart pounding, difficulty sleeping, or feel agitated, anxious, irritable or depressed)? ( ) YES ( ) NO

12. Count the number of "yes" answers. TOTAL YES: _____

    - 4 – 5 moderate opioid use disorder
    - 6 or more – severe opioid use disorder

The physician will need to select a diagnosis of moderate to severe opioid use disorder for coding purposes to treat this patient for OUD in the ER.

Appendix 2

CLINICAL OPIATE WITHDRAWAL SCALE (COWS)[2]

FOR EACH ITEM, CIRCLE the number that best describes the patient's signs or symptom. Rate on just the apparent relationship to opiate withdrawal. For example, if heart rate is increased because the patient was jogging just prior to assessment, the increased pulse rate would not add to the score.

Patient's Name: _____

Date and Time ___/___/___: _____

Reason for this assessment: _____

_____

Resting Pulse Rate: _____ beats/minute	GI Upset: *over last ½ hour*
Measured after patient is sitting or lying for one minute	0 no GI symptoms
0 pulse rate 80 or below	1 stomach cramps
1 pulse rate 81 – 100	2 nausea or loose stool
2 pulse rate 101 – 120	3 vomiting or diarrhea
4 pulse rate greater than 120	5 multiple episodes of diarrhea or vomiting

2. Wesson and Ling, *COWS*, 253–59.

Sweating: *over past ½ hour not accounted for by room temperature or patient activity* 0 no report of chills or flushing 1 subjective report of chills or flushing 2 flushed or observable moistness on face 3 beads of sweat on brow or face 4 sweat streaming off face	**Tremor** *observation of outstretched hands* 0 no tremor 1 tremor can be felt, but not observed 2 slight tremor observable 4 gross tremor or muscle twitching
Restlessness *Observation during assessment* 0 able to sit still 1 reports difficulty sitting still, but is able to do so 3 frequent shifting or extraneous movements of legs/arms 5 unable to sit still for more than a few seconds	**Yawning** *Observation during assessment* 0 no yawning 1 yawning once or twice during assessment 2 yawning three or more times during assessment 4 yawning several times/minute
Pupil size 0 pupils pinned or normal size for room light 1 pupils possibly larger than normal for room light 2 pupils moderately dilated 5 pupils so dilated that only the rim of the iris is visible	**Anxiety or Irritability** 0 none 1 patient reports increasing irritability or anxiousness 2 patient obviously irritable or anxious 4 patient so irritable or anxious that participation in the assessment is difficult
Bone or Joint aches *If patient was having pain previously, only the additional component attributed to opiates withdrawal is scored* 0 not present 1 mild diffuse discomfort 2 patient reports severe diffuse aching of joints/muscles 4 patient is rubbing joints or muscles and is unable to sit still because of discomfort	**Gooseflesh skin** 0 skin is smooth 3 piloerrection of skin can be felt or hairs standing up on arms 5 prominent piloerrection

Runny Nose or Tearing *Not accounted for by cold symptoms or allergies* 0 not present 1 nasal stuffiness or unusually moist eyes 2 nose running or tearing 4 nose constantly running or tears streaming down cheeks	Total Score: _____ The total score is the sum of all 11 items Initials of person completing assessment: _____

Score: 5–12 = mild; 13–24 = moderate; 25–36 = moderately severe; more than 36 = severe withdrawal

This version may be copied and used clinically.

Wesson, Donald R. and Walter Ling. *"The Clinical Opiate Withdrawal Scale (COWS)."* Journal of Psychoactive Drugs, 2003; 35(2), 253–259.

Reprinted by permission of Taylor & Francis Ltd, https://www.tandfonline.com.

Appendix 3

EMERGENCY DEPARTMENT MAT
INDUCTION ALGORITHM

Patient is identified with opioid use disorder and is in withdrawal.

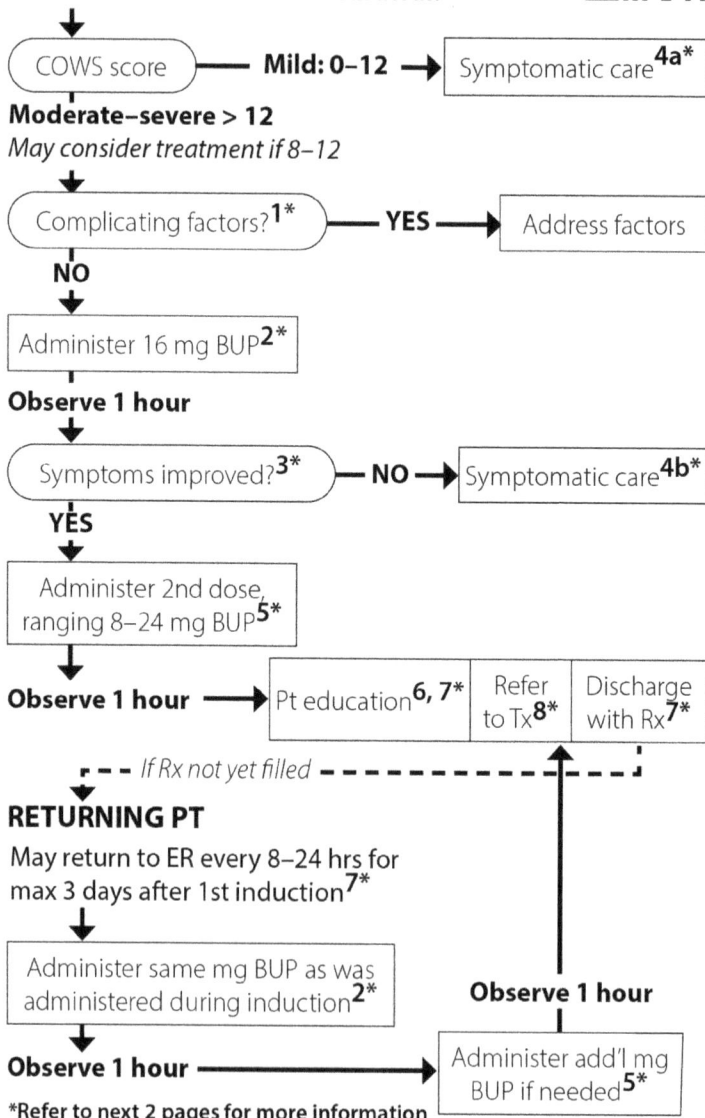

COWS score —— **Mild: 0–12** → Symptomatic care**4a***

Moderate–severe > 12
May consider treatment if 8–12

Complicating factors?**1*** —— **YES** → Address factors

NO

Administer 16 mg BUP**2***

Observe 1 hour

Symptoms improved?**3*** —— **NO** → Symptomatic care**4b***

YES

Administer 2nd dose, ranging 8–24 mg BUP**5***

Observe 1 hour → Pt education**6, 7*** | Refer to Tx**8*** | Discharge with Rx**7***

- - - *If Rx not yet filled* **- - - - - - - - - - - - - -**

RETURNING PT

May return to ER every 8–24 hrs for max 3 days after 1st induction**7***

Administer same mg BUP as was administered during induction**2***

Observe 1 hour → **Observe 1 hour**

Administer add'l mg BUP if needed**5***

*Refer to next 2 pages for more information

1. Complicating factors

   • Intoxicated or altered—check urine drug screen to identify fentanyl, alcohol, methamphetamine, etc., if patient cannot tell you what drug(s) are being used.

   • Pregnant—Buprenorphine is safe but methadone is not.

   • Taking methadone or long-acting prescription opioid—full withdrawal takes longer, up to 72 hours.

   • Chronic pain—history of taking prescribed opioids legally long-term.

   • If clinical suspicion of acute liver failure, check liver enzymes.

2. Dosing buprenorphine

   • Tailor dosing to the individual. Many have prior experiences with BUP—allow some degree of patient guidance. Maximum 24-hour dose is 64 mg for fentanyl users.

3. Consider precipitated withdrawal

   • BUP can cause withdrawal if too large a dose is given too soon. Should be 24–36 hours after last use.

4a. Symptomatic care

   • Consider clonidine, gabapentin, metoclopramide, low-dose ketamine, acetaminophen/NSAIDS.

   • Consider "Rx self-directed start" in *Appendix 4*; instructions are provided at top of middle column of *Emergency Department Buprenorphine (Bup) QuickStart.*

4b. Symptomatic care

   • Consider "If no improvement or worse . . ." in *Appendix 4*; instructions are provided in center of middle column of *Emergency Department Buprenorphine (Bup) QuickStart.*

5. Maximumdose is 64 mg on the first day

   • Recommended for heavy fentanyl users with high opioid tolerance.

6. Harm Reduction education

   • Dangers of benzo/alcohol co-use with BUP.

   • Keep BUP locked up at home.

- Narcan nasal spray kit for reversal of overdose at home.

7. DEA 72-hour dispensing rule or prescription given

- Pts may return to ED up to 3 consecutive days for repeated dispensing of BUP doses (needed in case Rx can't be filled in a timely fashion).

- Cost for BUP prescription:

  Health insurance or Medicaid—no co-pay but requires prior authorization.

  Cash—BUP 8/2 sublingual #21 about $125 for 7 days (if taken TID).

8. Out-patient treatment center in your community

- Patient needs to call for appointment (if you are unable to schedule for patient):

  Tel:(____)_____Mon-Fri hours:_____

EMERGENCY DEPARTMENT
BUPRENORPHINE (BUP) QUICK START

Emergency Department Buprenorphine (Bup) Quick Start

Connect with your patient: Accurate diagnosis and treatment requires trust, collaboration, and shared decision making.

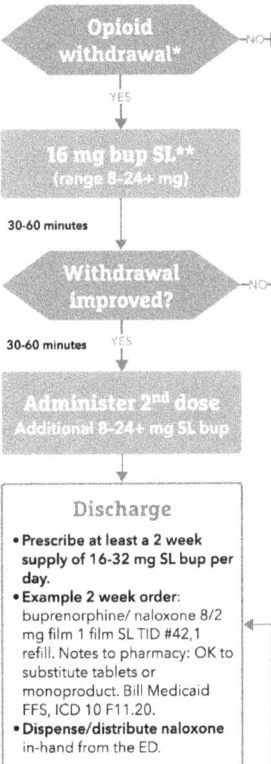

Opioid withdrawal* → NO →

Rx self-directed start:
- Wait for severe withdrawal then start with 8-24+ mg SL.
- Rx per "Discharge" box below.

YES ↓

16 mg bup SL** (range 8-24+ mg)

30-60 minutes ↓

Withdrawal improved? → NO →

30-60 minutes | YES ↓

Administer 2ⁿᵈ dose Additional 8-24+ mg SL bup

Discharge
- Prescribe at least a 2 week supply of 16-32 mg SL bup per day.
- Example 2 week order: buprenorphine/ naloxone 8/2 mg film 1 film SL TID #42,1 refill. Notes to pharmacy: OK to substitute tablets or monoproduct. Bill Medicaid FFS, ICD 10 F11.20.
- Dispense/distribute naloxone in-hand from the ED.

Bup Rx Notes
- The X-waiver program has ended. Only a DEA license is needed to prescribe (schedule III).
- Either bup or bup/nx SL films or tab are OK.
- Bup monoproduct or bup/nx OK in pregnancy.

For pregnancy: Bup in Pregnancy
For post-overdose: Bup Opioid Overdose

For minors: Caring for Youth
For self-directed starts: Bup Self Start

CA Bridge is a program of the Public Health Institute. © 2024, California Department of Health Care Services. Content available under Creative Commons Attribution NonCommercial NoDerivatives 4.0 International (CC BY-NC-ND 4.0).

If no improvement or worse, consider:

Worsening withdrawal (common): Occurs with lower starting doses and heavy tolerance; improves with more bup (additional 8-16 mg SL).

Other substance intoxication or withdrawal: Continue bup and manage additional syndromes.

Bup side-effects: e.g., nausea or headache. Continue bup and treat side-effects with supportive medications.

Medical illness: Continue bup and manage underlying condition.

If sudden & significant worsening, consider precipitated withdrawal (rare): See box below.

*Diagnosis Tips for Opioid Withdrawal:
1. Look for at least two clear objective signs not attributable to something else: large pupils, yawning, runny nose & tearing, sweating, vomiting, diarrhea, gooseflesh/piloerection, tachycardia.
2. Confirm with the patient that they feel 'bad' withdrawal and they feel ready to start bup. If they feel their withdrawal is mild, it is likely too soon.
3. As needed, consider using the COWS (clinical opioid withdrawal scale). Start if COWS ≥ 8 with ≥ 2 objective signs.
4. Withdrawal sufficient to start bup typically occurs 24-36 hrs after decreased/stopped use, but can vary from 6-72 hrs. Methadone withdrawal commonly takes longer.

**Bup Dosing Tips:
1. Respect patient preference. Shared decision making, flexibility, and collaboration are essential.
2. Heavy dependence/tolerance (e.g., fentanyl) may need higher doses of bup.
3. Low dependence/tolerance may do well with lower doses of bup.
4. Starting bup may be delayed or modified if there complicating factors:
   - Altered mental status, delirium, intoxication
   - Severe acute pain, trauma, or planned surgery
   - Severe medical illness
   - Long-term methadone maintenance

Treatment of bup precipitated withdrawal
(Sudden, significant worsening of withdrawal soon after bup administration.)

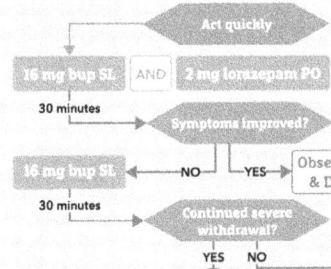

Act quickly

16 mg bup SL AND **2 mg lorazepam PO**

30 minutes ↓

Symptoms improved?

16 mg bup SL ← NO — YES → **Observe & DC**

30 minutes ↓

Continued severe withdrawal?

YES / NO

Escalate level of care to manage potential moderate to deep sedation including cardiac, pulse oximetry, and end tidal CO₂ monitoring:
1. Ketamine (0.3 mg/kg IV slow push q 15 minutes and/or infusion).
2. Fentanyl 200 mcg IV q10 minutes. Total dose of > 2000 mcg has been reported.

After clinical resolution, observe and discharge with bup Rx and/or XR-bup

Adjuvants:
OK but should not delay or replace bup. Use sparingly with appropriate caution.

Benzodiazepines:
- Lorazepam 2 mg PO/IV

Antipsychotics:
- Olanzapine 5 mg PO/IM

Alpha-agonists:
- Clonidine 0.1-0.3 mg PO

D2/D3 agonists:
- Pramipexole 0.25 mg PO

Gabapentinoids:
- Pregabalin 150 mg PO

California **Substance Use Line**
(844) 326-2626

Warmline (M-F 6am-5pm EST, Voicemail 24/7)
1-855-300-3595

CSAM CALIFORNIA SOCIETY OF ADDICTION MEDICINE | CAPA | CALIFORNIA ACEP | **June 2024**

REFERENCES

Emergency Department Buprenorphine (Bup) Quick Start

CA⌒
BRIDGE

CORRESPONDING AUTHOR

Andrew Herring, MD

AUTHORS

Erik Anderson, MD, Hannah Snyder, MD, Raul Ayala, MD, Arianna Campbell, PA-C, Bharath Chakravarthy, MD, Reb Close, MD, Alicia Gonzalez, MD, Gene Hern, MD, Andrew Herring, MD, Kevin Jones, MD, Kathy Lesaint, MD, Shahram Lotfipour, MD, Josh Luftig, PA-C, Aimee Moulin, MD, Leslie Mukau, MD, Edward Pillar, MD, Louis Tran, Rebecca Trotzky-Sirr, MD, Monish Ullal, MD, Jennifer Zhan, MD.

REFERENCES

Ang-Lee K, Oreskovich MR, Saxon AJ, et al. Single dose of 24 milligrams of buprenorphine for heroin detoxification: an open-label study of 5 inpatients. J Psychoactive Drugs. 2006 Dec;38(4): 505-512. doi: 10.1080/02791072.2006.10400589

Chambers LC, Hallowell BD, Zullo AR, Paiva TJ, Berk J, Gaither R, Hampson AJ, Beaudoin FL, Wightman RS. Buprenorphine dose and time to discontinuation among patients with opioid use disorder in the era of fentanyl. JAMA Netw Open. 2023;6(9):e2334540-e2334540

D'Onofrio G, O'Connor PG, Pantalon MV, et al. Emergency department-initiated buprenorphine/naloxone treatment for opioid dependence: a randomized clinical trial. JAMA. 2015 Apr 28;313(16): 1636–1644. doi:10.1001/jama.2015.3474

Greenwald MK, Herring AA, Perrone J, Nelson LS, Azar P. A neuropharmacological model to explain buprenorphine induction challenges. Ann Emerg Med. 2022

Greenwald MK, Comer SD, Fiellin DA. Buprenorphine maintenance and μ-opioid receptor availability in the treatment of opioid use disorder: implications for clinical use and policy. Drug Alcohol Depend. 2014;154:1-11. doi:10.1016/j.drugalcdep.2014.07.035

Herring AA, Perrone J, Nelson LS. Managing opioid withdrawal in the emergency department with buprenorphine. Ann Emerg Med. 2019;73(5): 481-487. doi: 10.1016/j.annemergmeed.2018.11.032

Hern GH, Lara V, Goldstein D, et al. Prehospital buprenorphine treatment for opioid use disorder by paramedics: first year results of the EMS buprenorphine use pilot. Prehosp Emerg Care, forthcoming. 2022. doi: 10.1080/10903127.2022.2061661

Kutz I, Reznik V. Rapid heroin detoxification using a single high dose of buprenorphine. J Psychoactive Drugs. 2001 Apr-Jun;33(2): 191-193. doi: 10.1080/02791072.2001.10400484

Jacobs P, Ang A, Hillhouse MP, et al. Treatment outcomes in opioid dependent patients with different buprenorphine/naloxone induction dosing patterns and trajectories. Am J Addict. 2015 Oct;24(7): 667–675. doi:10.1111/ajad.12288

Jones HE, Johnson RE, Lorraine Milio. Post-cesarean pain management of patients maintained on methadone or buprenorphine. Am J Addict. 2006 May-Jun;15(3)258-259. doi: 10.1080/10550490600626721

Liebschutz JM, Crooks D, Herman D, et al. Buprenorphine treatment for hospitalized, opioid-dependent patients: a randomized clinical trial. JAMA Intern Med. 2014 Aug;174(8): 1369–1376. doi:10.1001/jamainternmed.2014.2556

REFERENCES: Emergency Department Buprenorphine (Bup) Quick Start

More resources available www.cabridge.org

REFERENCES

Emergency Department Buprenorphine (Bup) Quick Start

CA
BRIDGE

Suarez EA, Huybrechts KF, Straub L, Hernández-Díaz S, Jones HE, Connery HS, Davis JM, et al. Buprenorphine versus methadone for opioid use disorder in pregnancy. N Engl J Med. 2022;387(22):2033-2044

Oreskovic MR, Saxon AJ, Ellis MLK, Malte CA, Roux JP, Knox PC. A double-blind, double-dummy, randomized, prospective pilot study of the partial mu opiate agonist, buprenorphine, for acute detoxification from heroin. Drug Alcohol Depend. 2005 Jan 7;77(1): 71-79. doi: 10.1016/j.drugalcdep.2004.07.008

Snyder H, et al. High-dose buprenorphine initiation in the emergency department among patients using fentanyl and other opioids. JAMA Netw Open. 2023;6(3):e231572

Walsh SL, Preston KL, Stitzer ML, Cone EJ, Bigelow GE. Clinical pharmacology of buprenorphine: ceiling effects at high doses. Clin Pharmacol Ther. 1994 May;55(5): 569-580. doi: 10.1038/clpt.1994.71

Weimer MB, Herring AA, Kawasaki SS, Meyer M, Kleykamp BA, Ramsey KS. ASAM Clinical considerations: Buprenorphine treatment of opioid use disorder for individuals using high-potency synthetic opioids. J Addict Med. 2023;10(7):e1097

Appendix 5

EMERGENCY DEPARTMENT AUTHORIZATION TO DISCLOSE PROTECTED HEALTH INFORMATION

Patient Name: _____

Date of Birth: _____ Phone # _____

Street Address: _____

City: _____ State: _____ Zip Code: _____

Purpose of Request: Continuation of Care

I authorize release of the Emergency Department notes related to substance use disorder screening, evaluation and/or treatment to the following referral site for continuity of care purposes. I authorize the ER staff to communicate with the outpatient clinic listed below and the ER staff may gather information about my follow up within 90 days of referral from the following:

Name of facility: _____

Phone #: _____ Fax: _____

Address: _____

City: _____ State: ___ Zip Code: _____

Dates of Service range (month/day/year):

From: _____ to: _____

The following information includes drug and alcohol treatment records; only the items checked below will be released:

Description of Information to be released:	Communication Type Authorized:
___ **Emergency Department Medication Assisted Treatment Note (may include HIV/AIDS, Genetic, STD, Communicable Disease, Mental Health information)** ___ **Social Work evaluation Notes**	___ **Verbal** ___ **Written**

The signature below indicates my consent to disclose the above bolded information.

_____

Signature of Patient or Legal Representative

Requests will be processed within 72 hours.

1. I authorize the release of my medical record, including photographs.

2. This authorization is voluntary and the disclosure is made at my request.

3. If the organization authorized to receive the information is not a health plan or health care provider, the released information may no longer be protected by federal privacy regulation.

4. I understand that this release will expire one year form the date signed unless I provide notice sooner that it should be revoked. Multiple requests are authorized if the purpose of the request remains the same.

5. I have a right to revoke this authorization at any time and if I revoke this authorization, I must do so in writing and present the written revocation to the department that I have authorized to release the information. Any revocation will not apply to information that has already been released in response to this authorization.

6. I need not sign this form to ensure health treatment.

I request this authorization to expire on _____, or one year from the date signed below and **covers only treatment for the dates specified above.** I am also aware fees, outlined below, for copy services may apply.

IMPORTANT WARNING: The documents accompanying this message are intended for the use of the person or entity to which this message is addressed. These documents may contain information that is privileged and confidential, the disclosure of which is governed by applicable law.

Unauthorized re-disclosure or failure to maintain confidentiality could subject you to penalties described in Federal Law (42 C.F.R., Part 2) and State Law. If you are the employee or agent responsible to deliver this information to the unintended recipient, you are hereby notified that any dissemination, distribution or copying this information is STRICTLY PROHIBITED.

———————————————————————

Name of Patient or Legal Representative

———————————————————————

Signature of Patient or Legal Rep

——————————

Date/Time

———————————————————————

Name of Staff Member

———————————————————————

Signature of Staff Member

——————————

Date/Time

Appendix 6

SUBOXONE INDUCTION DISCHARGE INSTRUCTIONS

WHAT IS BUPRENORPHINE?

Buprenorphine is a medication that is used to treat opioid addiction including addiction to heroin, fentanyl, counterfeit pill, los perc's, and prescription pills. It comes in several forms, the most common of these is a brand of buprenorphine combined with naloxone that is called Suboxone.

BUPRENORPHINE + NALOXONE = SUBOXONE

HOW DOES BUPRENORPHINE WORK?

Buprenorphine can treat withdrawal and reduce cravings by working on the same opioid receptors in the brain that were affected when using the opioids. It will make you feel normal, without a high and is NOT the same as substituting one addiction for another.

Buprenorphine if taken correctly can help lead to a healthy and productive life. It can help stabilize your brain while you focus on our own recovery, social functioning and improve your quality of life. There is no timeline for how long buprenorphine must be prescribed. Some people may have to take it life-long.

THE PRESCRIPTION FOR BUPRENORPHINE

You may have received a prescription for buprenorphine from the ER. It usually comes in films combined with naloxone. Please read the administration instructions carefully. You must be in withdrawal when you first start taking Suboxone, otherwise you can experience a severe form of withdrawal.

AFTER THE FIRST PRESCRIPTION FROM THE ER, KEEP ON GETTING TREATMENT IN A CLINIC

You will be given either an appointment in the local clinic before leaving the ER or you will have to contact the clinic yourself to set up your first appointment. Please make sure you keep that appointment at the clinic so that you don't have to go into withdrawal again. Bring your insurance information to that appointment and the prescription bottle. Most clinics will also provide information for you to have an appointment with their own therapist or they will link you with behavioral health to assist you as you make the important transition to a life of sobriety. The ER is open 24 hours a day, every day. Please return if you need further care.

DENTAL AND ORAL HEALTH MAINTENANCE

Rinse your mouth with water and then swallow completing this several times, after taking Suboxone. This will help protect your teeth and gums from developing abnormalities that can occur when this dissolved medication stays on your teeth and gums too long. Remember to get dental hygiene appointments regularly for the safety of your oral health.

Appendix 7

SAMPLE PRESCRIPTION
FOR BUPRENORPHINE/NALOXONE

Patient Name: _____

Date of Birth: _____

Address: _____

Suboxone 8/2 sublingual film
Place film under tongue until it dissolves BID for 7 days
#14 (fourteen)
No refills
Note: please substitute for different formulations as needed by insurance
Indication: Opioid Use Disorder (F11.20)

Prescriber Name: _____

Signature of Prescriber: _____

DEA #_____

NPI # _____

BIBLIOGRAPHY

"Buprenorphine Quick Start Protocol for EDs." www.cabridge.org.

Carroll, Gerard. "Emergency Response to Overdose and Treatment Panel." National Overdose Prevention Leadership Summit, Free Virtual Event, November 16–17, 2023. www.overdoseleadershipsummit.org.

Case, Anne, and Angus Deaton. *Deaths of Despair and the Future of Capitalism*. Princeton & Oxford: Princeton University Press, 2020.

Centers for Medicare & Medicaid Services. "Emergency Medical Treatment and Labor Act (EMTALA). Accessed April 27, 2024. www.cms.gov.

Fishman, Scott M. *Responsible Opioid Prescribing. A Guide for Michigan Physicians*. Washington DC: Waterford Life Sciences, 2007.

Hampton, Ryan. *Inside the Opioid Addiction Crisis and How to End It. American Fix*. New York: All Points Books, 2018.

Herring, Andrew, et al. "Emergency Department Access to Buprenorphine for Opioid Use Disorder." *JAMA Network Open*. 2024:7(1)e2353771. doi:10.1001/jamanetworkopen.2023.53771. Accessed 2/16/2024.

Hinz-Penner, Raylene. *East of Liberal: Notes on the Land*. Telford, Pennsylvania: Cascadia, 2022.

Hochstetler, Andrew and David Peters. "Why the Concern Over Opioids?" Community presentation in January, 2020 from Iowa State University, Department of Sociology and Criminal Justice; 2017 data.

Hoig, Stan. *The Sand Creek Massacre*. Norman: University of Oklahoma Press, 1961.

Interlandi, Jeneen. "Opinion: 48 Million Americans Live with Addiction. Here's How to Get Them Help That Works." *The New York Times*. https://www.nytimes.com/2023/12/13/opinion/addiction-policy-treatment-opioid.html.

Janzen, Jean. *Piano in the Vineyard*. "Child Diving." Intercourse, Pennsylvania: Good Books, 2004.

Lynch, William Jr. "Xylazine—What Is Happening Now." National Overdose Prevention Leadership Summit, Free Virtual Event, November 16–17, 2023. www.overdoseleadershipsummit.org.

McGinty, Emma E., and Colleen L. Barry. "Stigma Reduction to Combat the Addiction Crisis—Developing an Evidence Base." *NEJM* 382 (2020) 1291–92.

Nelson, Lewis. "Challenges and Understanding in Treatment." National Overdose Prevention Leadership Summit, Free Virtual Event, November 16–17, 2023. www.overdoseleadershipsummit.org.

Olorunnipa, Toluse, and Griff Witte. "Born with Two Strikes—Long Before George Floyd's Death, Systemic Racism Stifled His Life." *The Washington Post.* October 8, 2020.

Quinones, Sam. *Dreamland: The True Tale of America's Opiate Epidemic.* New York: Bloomsbury, 2015.

———. *The Least of Us: True Tales of America and Hope in the Time of Fentanyl and Meth.* New York: Bloomsbury, 2021.

Rotondo, Michael F., et al. *Advanced Trauma Life Support Student Course Manual, 9th ed.* American College of Surgeons Committee on Trauma. Chicago: American College of Surgeons, 2012.

Shaw, Gina. "No Excuses for Not Prescribing Buprenorphine in the ED: Buprenorphine Fits with EM's Mission to Help Patients When No One Else Will—and It Saves Lives." *Emergency Medicine News* 45(9) 16–17 (September, 2023). http://journals.lww.com/em-news/.

Suarez, E.A. et al. "Buprenorphine versus Methadone for Opioid Use Disorder in Pregnancy." *NEJM* 387 (2022) 2033–44.

Volkow, Nora D. "Stigma and the Toll of Addiction." *NEJM* 382 (2020) 1289–90.

Wells, David Wallace. "ESSAY: It's Not 'Deaths of Despair' It's Death of Children." *JAMA* (March 2023).

Wesson, Donald R., and Walter Ling. "The Clinical Opiate Withdrawal Scale (COWS)." *Journal of Psychoactive Drugs* 35:2 (2003) 253–259. https://doi.org/10.1080/02791072.2003.10400007.

Woodard, Colin. *American Nations: A History of the Eleven Rival Regional Cultures of North America.* New York: Penguin, 2011.

Court Documents, public domain.

"Initiating Buprenorphine Treatment in the ED." NIDA.nih.gov. March 17, 2023.

"Madonna of the Trail." Santa Fe Trail—Scenic and Historic Byway. Colorado's National Old Trails Road.

NOAA National Climatic Data Center. www.currentresults.com. "Average Annual Precipitation by State (USA), line 6. Accessed April 27, 2024.

"Questions for Identification of Opioid Use Disorder Based on DSM-5." https://www.nida.nih.org. Updated September 11, 2018. Accessed 4/27/2024.

www.ingramcontent.com/pod-product-compliance
Lightning Source LLC
Chambersburg PA
CBHW060342100426
42812CB00003B/1099